Practical Spirituality

According to

the Desert Fathers

By: Fr Athanasius Iskander

St Shenouda Coptic Orthodox Monastery

Putty, NSW, Australia

Title: Practical Spirituality According to the Desert Fathers
Author: Father Athanasius Iskander
Email: athanas@sympatico.ca

First Edition 2005

Published by: Saint Mary's Coptic Orthodox Church
Kitchener, Ontario, Canada
www.stmarycoptorthodox.org

Second Edition 2008

Published by: St Shenouda Coptic Orthodox Monastery
8419 Putty Rd Putty, N.S.W. 2330
Sydney, Australia
ISBN: 978-0-9805171-1-8

Cover Design: Marie Khairy
Cover Illustration: A Solitary Monk walking up to his cave
in the Egyptian Eastern Desert

The second edition was published with the kind permission of
Father Athanasius Iskander

TABLE OF CONTENTS

INTRODUCTION

The Book of Genesis tells us that man was created in the image of God. It is because of this that man has a natural tendency to seek God, in Whose image he was created.

Man was also created in the likeness of God. That means (among other things) in the likeness of the goodness of God. That means man was created with the tendency to be good, in the likeness of God Himself, the author of goodness. This intrinsic force that drives man to be good is sometimes called "The natural law" (Rom 2:14).

When Adam and Eve fell, human nature became fallen. Sin was introduced into the human nature. Sin made significant changes (for the worse) in man's will and intellect (mind). The will that was created with a God-seeking affinity became corrupted. Sin introduced self-seeking into the will of man. This led into a duality of will, a higher will, still seeking God, and a lower will that seeks after self gratifications.

Sin also corrupted the human mind, introducing "another law of sin" (Rom 7:23) that wars against the natural law of goodness. This led to a frustrating situation that St. Paul describes very well in Romans 7:18-19: "For I know that in me (that is, in my flesh) nothing good dwells; for to will is present with me, but how to perform what is good I do not find. For the good that I will to do, I do not do; but the evil I will not to do, that I practice.

When our Lord was incarnate, and took unto Himself the flesh of our weakness, uniting His divinity to our humanity, He elevated the human fallen nature to its original state, the state of the image and likeness of Him. And when He died on the Cross, He put an end to the dominance of sin on human nature. Our Lord gave us a chance to fight back to regain our original nature, by participating in His victory over sin and death through Holy Baptism.

Born again in Baptism, we receive the Holy Spirit which dwells in us, and works in us (and with us) through grace and helps us in the life-long struggle to restore our nature to the likeness of God once more. "Therefore you shall be perfect, just as your Father in heaven is perfect." Thus tells us the Lord in Matt 5:48. Having renewed us through Baptism, and sanctified us through the Holy Spirit, the Lord encourages us to seek perfection, even the perfection of our Father which is in heaven. This is the true meaning of regaining our likeness to God, and the ultimate goal of the restoration of our nature; Christian perfection. The reward for this is our return to Paradise, out of which we were driven out when we lost this God-like perfection.

The Bible tells us, in so many words, what we need to do to reach this perfection. When a young man came to our Lord asking Him, "What good thing shall I do that I may have eternal life?" (Matt 19:16) The Lord answered him, "Keep the commandments ... You shall not murder, You shall not commit adultery, You shall not steal, You shall not bear false witness, Honor your father and your mother, and, You shall love your neighbor as yourself." (Matt 19:17-19) When the man told the Lord that he has already kept all of these, the Lord told him, "If you want to be perfect, go, sell what you have and give to the poor, and you will have treasure in heaven; and come, follow me." (Matt 19:21) By this, the Lord was telling this young man, that the perfection of the Law, or those who think that they are fulfilling the Law (of Moses), like the Pharisees, cannot attain to the Heavenly Kingdom that our Lord has promised those who attain to the true Christian perfection, a level of perfection the young man was unwilling to reach for.

Although the Bible tells us WHAT we need to do to reach perfection (and earn Eternal Life,) it does not tell us HOW to reach perfection. It leaves it up to each one of us. "Work out your own salvation with fear and trembling," is what St Paul tells us in (Phil 2:12) It is quite obvious from this, that "Work" is an essential part of this process of salvation, according to the Bible. But, in this work we are not alone, we have a very strong ally in the grace of God, which works in us and with us through the Holy Spirit which dwells in us.

In the early years of the Church, Christians sought to work out their own salvation through offering the ultimate sacrifice; martyrdom. During the first three centuries, ten major persecutions gave millions of Christians their chance to strive for perfection. Shedding one's blood for the sake of Christ became the ideal of working out one's own salvation.

When Constantine became emperor and published his edict of toleration of Christianity (313 A.D.), Christians had to find another way of working out their own salvation. Many sought their own salvation in the wilderness. Unable to shed their blood for Christ's sake, they sought to offer Him their bodies as "a living sacrifice, holy, acceptable to God." (Rom 12:1) They took their clues from verses like, "And those who are Christ's have crucified the flesh with its passions and desires."(Gal 5:24) and "But I discipline my body and bring it into subjection, lest, when I have preached to others, I myself should become disqualified." (1 Cor 9:27) Other verses speak of this road to perfection as an athletic contest, "Do you not know that those who run in a race all run, but one receives the prize? Run in such a way that you may obtain it." (1 Cor 9:24) and, "let us run with endurance the race that is set before us." (Heb 12:1)

Other verses still speak of this quest for perfection as a war, "You have not yet resisted to bloodshed, striving against sin." (Heb 12:4) and, "You therefore must endure hardship as a good soldier of Jesus Christ. No one engaged in warfare entangles himself with the affairs of this life, that he may please him who enlisted him as a soldier." (2 Tim 2:3-4). Other images of this strife likened it to wrestling with beasts, "Be sober, be vigilant; because your adversary the devil walks about like a roaring lion, seeking whom he may devour." (1 Pet 5:8)

But the image that really fired their imagination was the image of a fight with the demons, the princes of darkness, "For we do not wrestle against flesh and blood, but against principalities, against powers, against the rulers of the darkness of this age, against spiritual hosts of wickedness in the heavenly places." (Eph 6:12) Those athletes of Christ went into the wilderness, to wrestle with the demons, in order to attain Christian perfection. Soon enough, monasticism took the place of martyrdom as the ideal of Christian perfection. In trying to work out their own salvation, those athletes of Christ did the rest of us a great favour. They left us a huge body of writings about how to attain Christian perfection.

The desert of Egypt became a university of this quest for spiritual perfection. The Desert Fathers made a science out of this quest for perfection that we now call spirituality. In this university research was done and experiments conducted, with either success or failure. Results of these experiments, whether they ended in success or failure, were published by many who came to seek the wisdom of the Desert Fathers.

The Fathers themselves never wrote their sayings, and spoke to others about their experiences only when they were constrained to do so. The Desert Fathers catalogued the sins, and the factors that predisposed them, and spoke in great detail on how to fight against them. They identified the various virtues, and classified them, giving exact techniques for attaining them.

The amazing thing about the sayings of the Desert Fathers is their agreement. While some lived in the Eastern desert, others in the Western desert (Scetis) and yet others in Upper Egypt, they reached the same conclusions. It is this unanimity of opinion that is most striking about these sayings. The differences are only in technique. The two most important characteristics of the spirituality of the Desert Fathers are as follows:

The first is their insistence on discipleship. Anyone seeking to learn the art of spirituality had to attach himself to a "master." This was not an easy matter, for those "masters" had very stringent "qualifying exams" for the candidates. St. Pachomius was left begging for three days outside the door of St. Palaemon's cell before being accepted as an apprentice! Books about these great saints usually say that he "trained with Abba ....."

Of course there were pioneers like St. Paul the Anchorite, St. Anthony the father of Monasticism and St. Macarius the great; men who laid the first foundations of this science, and who became founders of this university for the study of spirituality.

The second important rule was total avoidance of relying on one's self. The apprentice had to offer complete and blind obedience to the "master" who assumed total responsibility for training the novice. The masters tested the obedience of their disciples in many ways that would seem absurd to us! Like the master who gave his disciple a stick and ordered him to water it! Of course the obedience was not in vain, for after three years, the stick started to bud and bring fruits! Another novice, when he complained that there was a hyena nearby, was told by his master, catch it and bring it to me. In blind faith he went after the hyena and brought it back to the master only to be told, "Take it back, I told you to bring a hyena not a dog!"

Those who followed these rules faithfully, completed their training to become masters in their own right, teaching others what they had learned from their masters. A common thread, through the sayings of the Desert Fathers, is the statements like this, "Abba ... said that the blessed Abba ... used to tell him ...." A disciple propagated the sayings of his master not his own. Later on his disciples will propagate his own sayings and so on.

As fascinating as they are, the sayings of the Desert Fathers are not suitable for everyone. St. Paul tells the Corinthians in 1 Corinthians 3:2, "I fed you with milk and not with solid food; for until now you were not able to receive it, and even now you are still not able" For beginners to use these sayings is like giving a grownup's food to a baby.

There are many books written about spirituality, based on the sayings of the Desert Fathers. John Climacus book "The Ladder of Divine Ascent" and John Cassian's two books "The Institutes" and "The Conferences" are examples of such books.

A sixteenth century Russian Orthodox Abbot named Theophan the Recluse made a significant contribution to spirituality by collating many of the sayings of the Desert Fathers under some headings, and adding his own personal comments on how to implement their instructions and imitate their way of life. Again, this is a book written by a monk for monks.

"The Way of the Ascetics" is an exception to the above. It was written by a married Orthodox Christian living in Europe (Finland) in the first half of the twentieth century. It is a wonderful book that applies the methods of the Desert Fathers to ordinary people living in the world. It is a book that I recommend for anyone seeking to work out his or her own salvation.

However, as anyone knows, life in the middle of the twentieth century is so different from life in the twenty first century. The morals are different and the challenges are different.

The world is changing for the worse on a daily basis.

We need to borrow the methods and techniques of the Desert Fathers and apply them to the struggles faced by young Orthodox people living in the twenty first century.

This booklet is an attempt in that direction. It is based on sermons I gave to the youth of our church in Kitchener, Ontario, during the Lent of 2001. Most of them were later published in our periodical "Parousia". I also found out that the audio for these sermons is available on the Internet, no doubt the work of some of our over-zealous youth!

A word of caution to our readers: this book is not intended to be a "do it yourself manual" for spirituality. So, before you start to apply what is written, please consult your father in confession. Some of the exercises may not be suitable for you, and only your father in confession can give you the right advise in this regard.

The first step in the pursuit of Christian perfection is to re-align the will and the mind towards returning to the image and likeness of God. Chapters one and two deal with this discipline of the mind and the will. The next three chapters are concerned with the moral discipline; the fight against sins. Sins of the senses, sins of memory and imagination are touched upon, then a chapter is devoted to the presumptuous sins or the "hidden sin." The last part of the series deals with some of the essential virtues needed to start on the way of spiritual perfection.

May the Lord use this book for the glory of His Name.

Father Athanasius Iskander

Feast of the Presentation to the Temple

Mechir 8, 1721

February 15, 2005

CHAPTER ONE

DISCIPLINE OF THE MIND

Protect your Mind from Harmful and Unprofitable Knowledge:

If you wish to pursue Christian perfection, you have to protect your mind from information that is unprofitable to your soul. Unfortunately this is the age of information and information technology and the world is offering it to us like never before, an explosion of information through TV, books, magazines, newspapers and last but not the least, the Internet. But this leads to what I call pollution of the mind with useless information. Today we have information junkies, people who seek information, not to improve their efficiency at work, but information for its own sake.

St. Paul writing in 1 Corinthians 2:2 tells us, "For I determined not to know anything among you except Jesus Christ and him crucified." That is all the knowledge that St. Paul cares about, Jesus and his life- giving crucifixion. Ecclesiastes 1:18 tells us, "For in much wisdom is much grief, and he who increases knowledge increases sorrow."

The first example of unprofitable knowledge is excessive watching of the news. It is good to know what is happening in the world around us, but to be obsessed about knowing all the minute details of something happening somewhere else is not profitable if you are seeking Christian perfection. TV stations, responding to people's insatiable appetite for news have invented the 24 hour news channel. Radio channels followed suit!

Take an example, the proceedings of the O. J. Simpson trial were watched by more people around the world than any other event. I can understand watching a hockey game for example, but court proceedings? What could I possibly get out of it? Nothing that is profitable to my soul, mind or body!

Let me tell you about an exercise that I do during Lent, I refuse to listen to news on Radio, or read newspapers or magazines. Of course, we agreed that TV is not going to be operational during Lent. Believe me, I don't miss anything, rather my mind is freed from the information pollution, and I feel that it functions better.

We are told a story of a monk who was sitting chatting with the other monks, then, going to his cell; another monk saw him circling around his cell several times, so he asked him what he is doing He answered, "I am getting rid of all the worldly talk we were talking about, because I don't want to bring it in with me into my cell!"

The second example of unprofitable knowledge is idle curiosity. Seeking information about many things for the sole purpose of becoming knowledgeable! How can this hurt me? Well, the Fathers say that this glut of general knowledge, leads me to think that I know more than others and this leads to pride and arrogance. It also leads to talkativeness, because I want to parade my knowledge in front of others. Theophan the Recluse tells us that ultimately our mind becomes an idol which we worship. We ultimately become opinionated, refuse to consult or accept advise, since we know it all! This is pride of the mind which leads us to depend on ourselves even in spiritual matters, which is very dangerous.

If you want to follow after Christian perfection, you have to wean your mind from this addiction to knowledge. St. Paul says, in 1Corinthians 3:18-19, "If anyone among you seems to be wise in this age, let him become a fool that he may become wise. For the wisdom of this world is foolishness with God." Spiritual wisdom and worldly wisdom do not go hand in hand. People who seek after the wisdom of this world in an excessive way often become atheists. Puffed up by their own conceited minds they deny God who created their minds. Of these St. Paul says, in 1 Timothy 6:20-21 "O Timothy! Guard what was committed to your trust, avoiding the profane and idle babblings and contradictions of what is falsely called knowledge by professing it some have strayed concerning the faith. Grace be with you. Amen."

In Psalm 73:22-24 David the prophet says, "I was so foolish and ignorant; I was like a beast before you. Nevertheless I am continually with you; you hold me by my right hand. You will guide me with your counsel, and afterward receive me to glory." This is the meaning of becoming foolish in order to be wise. If you declare your foolishness before God, He will hold your right hand, guide you with His counsel, and afterwards receive you to Glory.

Curiosity led Lot's wife to perish. And the Lord gives us the same example in warning us about curiosity in the time of Antichrist. In Matthew 24:15-18 the Lord tells us, "Therefore when you see the abomination of desolation, spoken of by Daniel the prophet, standing in the holy place (whoever reads, let him understand), then let those who are in Judea flee to the mountains. Let him who is on the housetop not go down to take anything out of his house. And let him who is in the field not go back to get his clothes."

What this means is to avoid meeting or seeing or hearing the Antichrist at any cost, just to flee from him. People with very strong curiosity who just want to take a look, will perish just like Lot's wife. Luke 17:31-32 tells us the same thing and warns us not to fall in the mistake of Lot's wife. "In that day, he who is on the housetop, and his goods are in the house, let him not come down to take them away. And likewise the one who is in the field, let him not turn back. Remember Lot's wife."

In those days, one should curb any curiosity to watch TV, listen to the Radio, go to his "Revival Meetings" or any curiosity to know anything about him. St. John Chrysostom warns us, "He did not say, 'Go, and do not believe;' but, 'Go not forth, neither depart thither.' For great then will be the deceiving, because that even deceiving miracles are wrought." If you ignore these warnings and follow your curiosity you will be deceived and will perish. That is why it is good to exercise yourself in fasting from TV during Lent so that should the time of Antichrist come upon us, we can get rid of our TV altogether and keep our eyes fixed on heaven waiting for the coming of the Lord on the clouds to gather us unto Him. Another deadly kind of curiosity is curiosity about the Occult, Witchcraft, Ouija boards and the like, which can lead to demonic possession and suicide or murder.

So far we have spoken about unprofitable knowledge, now let us talk about harmful knowledge. This is obsession with knowing things about other people, or what the Bible calls being a busybody. 1 Peter 4:15 tells us, "But let none of you suffer as a murderer, a thief, an evildoer, or as a busybody in other people's matters."

Obsession about knowing the affairs of others is the root of gossip. The devil may convince you that you want to know those things so that you can help the other person. But, I can pray for a sick person without knowing about the kind of illness he has. I can help someone move into his new house without prying into how much he paid for the house. I can congratulate someone for his new job without asking him how much salary he is getting. Young people especially are obsessed by knowing the "secrets" of their friends. If you don't tell me your secrets then you are not my friend. Or, I'll tell you my secrets if you tell me yours. This is harmful knowledge and the Bible tells us that being a busybody is as bad as being a murderer or a thief. Many people complain to me about other people wanting to know things about them. Some people even tell me, "I have to lie sometimes because I don't want people to know my personal affairs." My standard answer is, "Don't lie, just tell those people, this is personal!" And if they get upset and don't want to talk to you anymore, don't worry for they are not true friends any way.

True friends respect the privacy of their friends rather than insist on knowing their secrets.

Plant in your Mind the Spiritual Knowledge:

We all read the Bible and memorize verses, but do we implant these spiritual principles that the verses contain in our minds? In Deuteronomy 6: 6- 9 we are told, "And these words which I command you today shall be in your heart. You shall teach them diligently to your children, and shall talk of them when you sit in your house, when you walk by the way, when you lie down, and when you rise up. You shall bind them as a sign on your hand, and they shall be as frontlets between your eyes. You shall write them on the doorposts of your house and on your gates". That means that we have to assimilate what we read in the Bible and imprint them in our hearts and minds, until they become part of our thought process. Here are some examples:

The Bible tells us in Luke 6:26 "Blessed are you when men hate you, and when they exclude you, and revile you, and cast out your name as evil, for the Son of Man's sake. Rejoice in that day and leap for joy! For indeed your reward is great in heaven". According to this, to be despised is more blessed than to be praised. Have I implanted in my mind that when people praise me this is dangerous for my spiritual perfection, and when they despise me and say evil things against me falsely, I am blessed? You may say that this is impossible but it has been done.

Bishop Youannis of blessed memory used to go every Thursday to preach in a nearby village. As it is usual in Egypt he had to share a cab with some other people to go to that village. It so happened that a fanatic Moslem used to take the same cab at the same time on Thursdays, and as soon as Bishop Youannis would enter the cab, he would turn the other way and spit! This went on for years. One day the Bishop went on the Taxi but the other guy did not come. Bishop Youannis felt grieved in his heart and started complaining to God, "Why did you deprive me of this blessing Lord? Is it on account of my many sins that you decided that I am no more worthy of this blessing?" Another Bishop of blessed memory was Bishop Samuel, who was a tireless worker for the Lord, and as usual he had many enemies, people who hated him and sent him very nasty letters. He kept these nasty letters in a drawer. Each time he felt discouraged or cast down, he would open the file and start reading the nasty letters and he would feel refreshed once again because he saw in each insult that he read in these letters a blessing. This is what we mean by implanting what we read in the Bible on our hearts.

The Fathers took training in accepting insults and rejecting praise very seriously. The book of the Paradise of the Fathers tells us two wonderful stories about this discipline of the mind. One Abba told a novice disciple, go and insult the dead! So, out of obedience, he went to the graveyard and started shouting insults at the dead for a whole day. The next day, his Abba told him, go and praise the dead. He went to the graveyard and started heaping praise on the dead. When he came back in the evening, his master asked him, "When you insulted the dead, did they feel it?" He said," No." Again he asked him, "When you praised the dead, did they feel it?" He answered, "No." The old man told him, "Go and be like this."

The other story is about a young man from a rich family who went into a monastery to become a monk. His Abba told him, "Train yourself in accepting insults with joy!" He looked around him, but there was no one to insult him in the monastery. So, he went to the village and hired a man to come to the monastery   to insult him, until he got really trained in accepting insults with joy.

One day, he was on an errand in the city, together with the other monks, when a mad man started hurling insults at

him and he started laughing! The other monks asked him why
he is laughing? He told them, "I used to pay for this, now I am
getting it for free!"

The Bible tells us in 1 John 2:15, "Do not love the world
or the things in the world. If anyone loves the world, the love
of the Father is not in him" and again in James 4:4, "Do you
not know that friendship with the world is enmity with God?
Whoever therefore wants to be a friend of the world makes
himself an enemy of God."

Have we implanted this in our minds? The way to perfection
is despising the world and all the things in the world. St. Paul
says in Philippians 3:8 "Yet indeed I also count all things loss
for the excellence of the knowledge of Christ Jesus my Lord,
for whom I have suffered the loss of all things, and count them
as rubbish, that I may gain Christ." St. Paul says I'd rather
lose everything to gain the knowledge of Christ, considering
all things of the world as rubbish. Garbage! Have you
implanted in your heart that this world is a big garbage can
and all the things in it are garbage? If I still look at a car and I
am spellbound with awe, is this car not becoming an idol that
I worship?

I remember one day I was giving a ride to a group of
young people, coming back from an activity, all the way from
Mississauga to Kitchener; all they talked about was cars. Have
you ever seen one of those big trucks that carry the carcasses
of cars, flattened into pieces of metal on the way to the dump?
Or have you ever seen a car dump? It looks ugly. Every time
you covet a car, tell your mind, in a few years this car will be
an ugly piece of metal sitting in an ugly car dump. Train your
mind to despise worldly things and to covet spiritual perfection.
The Bible tells us in Proverbs 16:32, "He who is slow to anger
is better than the mighty, and he who rules his spirit than he
who takes a city." Did I implant in my mind that controlling

my anger is actually strength and not weakness? It is easy to respond to angry words with angry words or to aggression with aggression, that is the easy way, the way of the weak. But to control your anger and not to respond in the same kind is the difficult way the way of the strong and the mighty. Have you implanted in your mind that turning the other cheek is not cowardice but is actually courage?   You tell me it can't be done, but I tell you it can.

This is a real story that happened in the nineties. A monk went out to Cairo to do some necessary repairs to some equipment belonging to the monastery. In one of the narrow streets of Cairo, the car he was driving scratched another car parked there. He enquired about the owner, apologized to him and offered to pay for the repairs. The owner was a fanatic, who saw a chance to vent his hatred towards Christians, so he started abusing the monk verbally then slapped him on the face. The monk simply turned the other cheek. The man was taken by surprise, he started crying and apologizing to the monk, telling him,

"They tell us that you are bad, but really, you are better than us!" The man asked the monk, what brings him to Cairo, and when he told him about the repairs needed, the man told him that he has a business for repairing this kind of equipment. Not only did he do the repairs for free, but he asked the monk to promise him that every time he needs repairs, he would go no where else.

St. Paul tells us in Philippians 1:23, "For I am hard-pressed between the two, having a desire to depart and be with Christ, which is far better." and again in Philippians 1:21, "For to me, to live is Christ, and to die is gain." Did I implant in my mind that death is actually a gain and not a loss? And that to depart and be with Christ is far better? Have I trained my mind to covet that which an eye has not seen, nor an ear has heard, neither have come upon the heart of man? Have I got the proper spiritual understanding of the true meaning of life and death?

CHAPTER TWO

DISCIPLINE OF THE WILL

St. Paul tells us in Romans 7:22-23 "For I delight in the law of God according to the inward man. But I see another law in my members, warring against the law of my mind, and bringing me into captivity to the law of sin which is in my members."

The Fathers tell us that this means that each one of us has in him two wills, a higher will, the inner man, which seeks after things that are, "above, where Christ is, sitting at the right hand of God." (Col 3:1), and a lower, sensual will or "the law of sin" which is in our members, that seeks after things of the world and the flesh. These two wills are at war with each other as St. Paul tells us in Romans 7:23.

Unfortunately the law of sin is most of the time victorious bringing into captivity the higher will. Needless to say that the sensual will or the lower will or the law of sin is under the direction of the devil, our arch-enemy, and the higher will is under the direction of Grace.

The goal of Christian perfection is to reverse the situation and bring the sensual will into captivity to the higher will, a difficult goal, even for St. Paul himself who laments this difficulty by saying, "O wretched man that I am! Who will deliver me from this body of death?" (Rom 7:24)

The devil is so clever, so if we even succeed in subjecting the lower will to the higher will, he changes his tactic, by trying to corrupt the higher will, making it function independently of Grace, so that even though we are doing good, this good is not according to the will of God and is done in a way not pleasing to God. Even if he fails in this, he tries another strategy, he plants pride and self righteousness in our hearts, thus robbing us of the rewards of any righteousness we may have.

I think by now we realize how vicious this war is! And we are expected to fight it till the last breath! St. Paul warns us in Hebrews 12:4, "You have not yet resisted to bloodshed, striving against sin." He also reminds us in Ephesians 6:12-13 "For we do not wrestle against flesh and blood, but against principalities, against powers, against the rulers of the darkness of this age, against spiritual hosts of wickedness in the heavenly places. Therefore take up the whole armor of God, that you may be able to withstand in the evil day, and having done all, to stand."

St. Peter also advises us, "Be sober, be vigilant; because your adversary the devil walks about like a roaring lion, seeking whom he may devour." (1 Pet 5:8) It is an uphill battle that we have to fight and are expected to win. You may say, this is very difficult. Well, the Lord Jesus agrees 100%, "Because narrow is the gate and difficult is the way which leads to life, and there are few who find it." (Matt 7:14) The good news, however, is that our adversary the devil, the roaring lion, cannot force our free will. He acts only as a clever salesman trying to sell us his wares. It is entirely up to us whether we accept the sales pitch or reject it.

When we first came to Canada, we were fooled many times by clever sales people who sold us many things that later turned out to be worthless. But with experience we learned not to believe everything a salesman tells us. With so many of them phoning us at the most inappropriate times and boring us with their promises, we have learned how to be tough with them, cut them short and not allow them to engage us in a discussion. Sometimes you have to be rude in order to get rid of them.

These people use various tricks to convince people to fall into their traps. We are all aware of this line, "Congratulations, you have just won a free trip to Jamaica" or a TV etc.. But if you are wise you can spoil their deceit. I personally tell them, it is against my religion to accept anything for free and then hang up.

It is the same with the devil, he will use tricks, very crafty tricks but if you insist on saying no he cannot do anything.

He will change his tactics like we said before but you can have victory in this war if you are sober and vigilant like St. Peter tells us.

How can I resist the sales pitches that the devil always throws against me? The first thing is through prayer. Bring your weakness to the Lord Jesus, say the prayer that we learned in the Agpeya, "If the righteous is hardly saved, where shall I the sinner stand? The burden of the day and its heat I could not bear because of my human frailty." Cry with St. Paul, saying, "Who will deliver me from this body of death" except you O my Lord. Say with the Psalmist, "Have mercy on me, O LORD, for I am weak" (Ps 6:2) . The devil can not prevail on someone who acknowledges his weakness before the Lord.

The second thing is to teach yourself how to hate sin and the salesman of sin, the devil. In the same way you have learned how to hate those annoying sales people who interrupt your dinner, learn how to hate sin and the devil. Remind yourself that the wages of sin is death and that sooner or later we shall all stand before the Judgement Seat of Christ. Repeat in your mind the words of the Agpeya, "Behold, I am about to stand before the Just Judge, frightened and terrified of my many sins."

Prayer and the remembrance of Judgement Day are your defence lines, but what can I do when the enemy attacks? Let us take an example: Suppose a person verbally abuses you. Immediately the salesman comes to you convincing you to defend your honour and not to let that jerk think that you are a sissy, and after all he started this and you are only acting in self defence. On and on goes the sales pitch. Your first reaction is to realize this as a Satanic sales pitch. Say to yourself, "wait a minute, this is a pitch to sell me the sin of anger and the other one of revenge". Diagnose the kind of sin you are being sold. Next, arrest it before it reaches your heart and starts to stir up your emotions. Drive it away by saying, "Get behind me

Satan". Do not think that the devil will listen and get behind you, he will bring the thought back as soon as you drive it out. Here is where the defences we spoke about earlier come into play. Train yourself to hate these suggestions and consider them your mortal enemies. Say with the Psalmist, "O daughter of Babylon, who are to be destroyed, happy the one who repays you as you have served us! Happy the one who takes and dashes your little ones against the rock!" (Ps 137:8-9, Septuagint.) The Fathers tell us that the children of the daughter of Babylon are the evil thoughts that assail us.

The Fathers of the Desert also teach us a certain prayer that they used a lot to fight these thoughts. It is the secret weapon that we can always use against the salesman and his sales pitches. It is the first verse of Psalm 70 (69 in the Septuagint) "Make haste, O God, to deliver me! Make haste to help me, O LORD!" There is a whole chapter in John Cassian's book "The Conferences" on the use of this secret weapon against these thoughts. Keep saying this prayer repeatedly in your mind until you regain your peace.

If you want to eradicate this thought completely, do the opposite to what the salesman is telling you to do; an act of charity towards this aggressor. To seek perfection does not mean only to eradicate the sin but also to plant a virtue in its place. This is what is meant in Psalm 34:14, "Depart from evil and do good; seek peace and pursue it." The Lord tells us the same thing, "Love your enemies, do good, ... and you will be sons of the most High. For he is kind to the unthankful and evil." (Luk 6:35)

It is needless to say that these exercises of the will can not be successful if we have not first mastered the exercises of the mind, we spoke about last week. Your mind must be trained to accept abuse trusting in what the Lord told us, "Woe to you when all men speak well of you", and, "Blessed are you when they revile and persecute you, and say all kinds of evil against you falsely… Rejoice and be exceedingly glad".

In spite of all of this, the war can be relentless and the thoughts can come upon us like the waves of the sea one after the other. To be able to fight back, you have to memorize some verses that you can use as your battle cry against your enemy, for example say with the Psalmist, "The LORD is my light and my salvation; whom shall I fear? The LORD is the strength of my life; of whom shall I be afraid? When the wicked came against me to eat up my flesh, my enemies and foes, they stumbled and fell. Though an army may encamp against me, my heart shall not fear; though war may rise against me, in this I will be confident." Psalm 27 (26 Coptic 1-3) Repeat this verse in your mind.

Also seek the help of the Virgin Mary, say the prayer we say in the Agpeya, "O pure Virgin cast the shadow of your protection on me, your servant. Keep away from me the waves of vile thoughts." These prayers of the Agpeya were put for us by the Fathers to help us in this war between the wills. If the thoughts keep assailing you always remember that those who are with us are more than those against us.

One day an evil king sent a whole army against Elisha the prophet of the Lord, and when his servant saw the chariots and the weapons surrounding them he feared greatly, but Elisha told him, "Do not fear, for those who are with us are more than those who are with them." And Elisha prayed, and said, LORD, I pray, open his eyes that he may see." Then the LORD opened the eyes of the young man, and he saw. And behold, the mountain was full of horses and chariots of fire all around Elisha." (2 Ki 6:16-17)

The same happened to St. Moses the Black. Evil thoughts kept assailing him and every time he went to his Father in Confession St. Isidore to tell him about the thoughts that were bothering him. After he has been there for 14 times, St. Isidore took him up to the top of his cell and told him "look to the west and tell me what you see?" He told him "I see demons throwing fiery darts against the monks." He told him now look to the east and what do you see?" He told him, "I see angels defending the monks against the demons' fiery darts." He asked him, "Who are more, those who assail us or those who defend us?" St. Moses told him, "those who defend us." Immediately the thoughts ceased to attack him.

Resisting the thoughts that the enemy implants into our minds is not without its rewards, as this story from the Fathers tells us; A young monk living with his Abba, was in the habit of never going to sleep before he prostrated himself before the Abba asking him to bless him. One night he came and prostrated himself and said, "Bless me Abba" but his Abba was fast asleep. He remained there, hoping that the Abba would wake up but the Abba kept sleeping all night long. It so happened that during his sleep, the Abba saw seven angels putting seven crowns on the head of his disciple. In the morning he asked the disciple, "What happened during the night?" The young monk said to him, "Forgive me Abba but during the night, seven times the thought came to me to leave you and go to bed, and every time I resisted the thought." The Abba then knew that the crowns were for resisting the thoughts. He told the story to the other monks but did not tell the young disciple, lest he should fall into pride.

We should always plant good thoughts instead of the evil ones that the salesman of evil plants in our minds. These are some examples of how we can do that:

If the devil offers you thoughts of murmuring and complaining, because you failed an exam or some mishap happened to you and he starts telling you it is not fair, fight them by saying "Thank you Lord." In the beginning you will be saying it by your tongue only but after a while your heart starts saying it along with your tongue.

If the sales pitch is thoughts of anger against someone who wronged you, oppose them by trying to invent excuses for that person. If the thoughts keep coming in waves fight them by saying, "Lord forgive him and forgive me."

One very important weapon in the fight against these sales pitches is to ask your father in confession to pray for you. Just phone him and tell him, "Abouna the salesman is almost convincing me, please help me with your prayers."

The book, The Paradise of the Fathers, tells us that a monk was sent by his father in confession to do an errand in the city, when he went into the house he was supposed to go to, a beautiful girl tried to entice him to sin with her, he immediately cried out, "Lord through the prayers of my father in confession please save me", and immediately he found himself on the road towards the Monastery.

CHAPTER THREE

DISCIPLINE OF THE SENSES

Theophan the Recluse likens man to a king (the soul) who lives in a castle (the body) The castle has 5 windows and a door. The 5 windows are the five senses. The door is the mind. The enemy, can not enter into the castle except through the windows or the door. If these are closed shut, the enemy can not enter into the castle.

Through these windows, the salesman of sin can bring in samples of different experiences or sensations that bring delights to the soul. Out of these, the soul bundles together a circle of comfort and pleasure (fun). The soul comes to consider this circle of pleasure as its primary good and goal. In this way, the order of things becomes inverted, and instead of seeking God and His Kingdom, the soul seeks "fun".

A person who seeks to start on the road of spiritual perfection, has to re-establish the original order of life; to find comfort in God and not in fun. Sometimes we take this decision, yet the struggle is long and difficult. After years of pleasing and pandering to one's self, it is very difficult to wean the soul from the bad habits it had acquired over the years. Disciplining the senses is crucial for success in this struggle to re-establish the normal order of things within oneself.

Each sense has its pleasant and unpleasant subjects. The soul delights in pleasurable things and, becoming addicted to them, always lusts after them. In this way, each sense introduces into the soul several lusts or passionate attachments. These lusts lie dormant in the soul until the object of lust is once again experienced by the sense. Once the lust is re-ignited within the soul, a chain reaction begins as St. James tells us in James1:15 "Then, when desire has conceived, it gives birth to sin; and sin, when it is full-grown, brings forth death." Now the saying of Jeremiah becomes fulfilled, "Death has come through our windows, has entered our palaces." (Jer 9:21) That is death has entered through the senses into the soul.

The discipline of the senses is twofold. Not only should we prevent our senses from wandering about and getting harmful impressions, but we should also train them to receive profitable impressions from every creature and everything.

Discipline of the Eyes:

There are many verses in the Bible that exhort us to discipline our eyes: "The lamp of the body is the eye. If therefore your eye is good, your whole body will be full of light. But if your eye is bad, your whole body will be full of darkness." (Matt 6:22-23) "If your right eye causes you to sin, pluck it out and cast it from you; for it is more profitable for you that one of your members perish, than for your whole body to be cast into hell." (Matt 5:29) "Whoever looks at a woman to lust for her has already committed adultery with her in his heart." (Matt 5:28)

In the old times keeping the eye pure was not very difficult. The commandment "Do not look upon a woman in lust" was not difficult to follow, for women in those days were properly dressed and mostly covered up. Today however it is very difficult to keep the eye from encountering offenses. Not only has the dress code become so offensive, but there are so many ways that the devil, the salesman of sin, can introduce impurity into the eyes.

Magazines and books are now filled with pornography, and it seems that society is gradually increasing its tolerance and indeed its desire for more and more explicit porn. You go shopping and while standing in line at the cashier, your eyes are bombarded with offensive pictures from every direction. Grocery stores now have candy free lanes, I wish they would introduce porn free lanes.

Department stores are not any better. The varieties of

intimate apparel that is on display and the way it is displayed makes it very difficult for the eyes to remain in their sockets. Even if you are just walking in a mall, the windows of many shops are filled with displays of intimate ware. As if this is not enough, some stores would exhibit those items worn by manikins. Billboards on public roads and public transportation are now showing a lot of material that offends the eye (or delights it, depending on whether your eye is single or evil.)

TV offers us a more animated version of the same. There is hardly a movie without some kind of porn in it, even cartoons. The Internet has now equaled or even surpassed TV in the amount and variety of sinful sights it offers, and they are only a mouse click away.

In trying to wean the eyes from the depraved scenes it became accustomed to, it is good to reflect on what the Bible tells us. The book of Genesis tells us that "the sons of God saw the daughters of men, that they were beautiful; and they took wives for themselves of all whom they   chose." (Gen 6:2). The results were disastrous, for we are then told, in Genesis 6: 7, "So the LORD said, I will destroy man whom I have created from the face of the earth." Looking and lusting after women led to the destruction of mankind.

The story of David should be a reminder to us of how dangerous it is for the eye to wander about without control. How carelessness about controlling the eyes has turned the author of the Psalms into an adulterer and a murderer.

One should struggle unto the blood against all of the above. It is very difficult, but absolutely necessary for our salvation. It is one thing to encounter these things while walking or shopping and another thing to seek them, by looking for them on TV or the internet, or even worse by renting pornographic videos or buying pornographic magazines. The punishment is much more for the latter than the former.

Watching violence is also another sin. There is hardly any movie now without violence. Even cartoons are filled with very violent scenes. Many sports are violent. There is hardly a hockey game without a delicious bit of banging and stumping. An even more dangerous is the so called "sport" wrestling. I know a few kids who are addicted to watching wrestling.

Parents should watch over their children and make sure that they are seeing only appropriate things for their ages. There are ways and means for preventing your children from watching porn on TV and the internet. You should investigate and install these things before getting the internet or cable into your house.

Looking with lust at foods and pictures of food is also to be avoided especially during fasting. Remember that this is what Eve did, "And when the woman saw that the tree was good for food, that it was pleasant to the eyes, ... she took of its fruit and ate." (Gen 3:6) The rest is history. Today we are bombarded by so many bigger than life pictures of hamburgers, Ice cream, and even Kit Kats that make any mouth water.

Looking with lust at other worldly things, cars, houses, furniture, clothes, computers, toys, etc.. , is another sin that we commit with the eyes. The Lord Jesus was tempted in this way when the salesman of sin showed Jesus "all the kingdoms of the world and their glory; And he said to Him, "All these things I will give You if You will fall down and worship me."" (Matt 4:8-9) The devil is still using the same trick trying to tempt us to covet earthly things. Jesus resisted the temptation by using verses of the Bible to answer Satan. We can do the same when he tries to tempt us, by remembering that "If anyone loves the world, the love of the Father is not in him." (1 Jn 2:15) And that "friendship with the world is enmity with God? Whoever therefore wants to be a friend of the world makes himself an enemy of God." (Jas 4:4)

The evil eye or the envious eye is another way the eye can offend us. To look with envy at what others have is a sin that we are warned against both in the Old and the New Testaments. The book of Job tells us that "Envy slays the simple one." Job 5:2

The parable of the householder, who went out early in the morning to hire labourers for his vineyard is an example of how envy is hated by God. Matthew 20:1-15 tells us that the man hired labourers and agreed on their wages. Then he went out and hired others who worked less but he gave them the same wages. Now those who worked for a full day complained that the householder gave those who worked less the same wages. It's not fair! But the householder told them, "Is it not lawful for me to do what I wish with my own things? Or is your eye evil because I am good?"

A question that is often put forward to me by many is, "How come those who are far away from God always get good things in their life?" The same thought came into the mind of the writer of Psalm 73, "I was envious of the boastful, when I saw the prosperity of the wicked. ... They are not in trouble as other men, nor are they plagued like other men. ... Their eyes bulge with abundance; they have more than heart could wish. ... Behold, these are the ungodly, who are always at ease; they increase in riches." God, responding to these nagging questions showed the Psalmist the end of the wicked, as we are told later in the Psalm, "I went into the sanctuary of God; then I understood their end. Surely you set them in slippery places; you cast them down to destruction. Oh, how they are brought to desolation, as in a moment! They are utterly consumed with terrors."

There is no unfairness with God. Those who choose not to work for eternal life get their portion in this life. We are told in Psalm 17:14-15, "Men of the world who have their portion in this life, and whose belly you fill with your hidden treasure. They are satisfied with children, and leave the rest of their possession for their babes. As for me, I will see your face in righteousness; I shall be satisfied when I awake in your likeness." The parable of the rich man and Lazarus is another example of this, when the rich man asked Abraham to "send Lazarus, that he may dip the tip of his finger in water, and cool my tongue; for I am tormented in this flame." Abraham answered him, "Son, remember that in your lifetime you received your good things, and likewise Lazarus evil things; but now he is comforted and you are tormented." Luke 16:24-25

The Proper Use of the Eyes:

One should not only train his eyes not to look with lust at anyone or anything but also should train the eyes to see God in everyone and in everything. We have many examples from the Fathers of the desert that show us how to do that. A monk was sent by his superior to Alexandria on an errand and when he came back the other monks asked him, "What is Alexandria like?" He simply answered them, "I did not purpose to look at anything in Alexandria." He went there to do some business and he had no wish to do any sight seeing!

We can train ourselves in the same manner, to look at things in simplicity. To see God in all creatures animate and inanimate. If I see a beautiful person of the other sex, instead of making him or her an object of lust, I should think of God the Creator Who made such a beautiful person. This is what Christ meant when He told us if your eye is good, your whole body will be full of light.

Similarly, if you see a beautiful home, remember your real home in the Heavenly Jerusalem. Tell yourself, if this house is so beautiful, how much more beautiful is the house "not built with hands" that the Lord is preparing for me? Repeat in your mind the word of the beautiful hymn, "Jerusalem my happy home, when shall I come to thee, When shall my woes come to an end, thy joys that I may see!" In a similar way, when you look at a car and say Wow! Meditate on how much more beautiful was the fiery chariot that took Elijah to heaven.

Another exercise the Fathers use, is using seen objects to meditate on the Passion of our Lord. For example, if you see a rope, meditate on how the Lord was bound for your sake. If you see a nail think of the nails that were put in his hands because of your sins.

Finally, what should I do if I inadvertently see something offensive? Delete it from your mind in the same way you delete objects from your computer! With an intense act of the will, blank the picture and delete it! This is perhaps what the Lord means by saying if your eye offends you pluck it out and throw it out. Take the offence out of your mind and dash it against the rock.

Discipline of the Ears:

Perhaps the most common offense to the ear is bad music, bad lyrics even blasphemous lyrics. Very loud and violent music is also to be avoided. I sometimes walk into a store to buy something, and I hate the music they are pumping into my ear. Some music gives me the feeling that the devil is beating the drums!

One of the most offensive media now is music videos. Not only are you bombarded by very lustful lyrics sung in a very lustful way, but your eyes are also bombarded with very lustful scenes. The results are devastating and they are all over the TV. Bad music often sticks to your mind and the words keep repeating themselves in your mind while you are working or walking or even while you are praying.

Another offense is hearing heretic talk or watching heretic programs on TV. I often look at and listen to "so-called" TV evangelists, and not one of them passes my stringent test of Orthodoxy. There is often nice words from the Bible that entice the simple and the uncritical, but there is always the poison hidden in the honey.

"Preachers" who think that they can explain the prophesies of the Bible are all over the waves. There are those who speak of the "Left behind" phantasy also known as the "Rapture heresy". This heresy is less than 150 years old, and it teaches that Christ will come to take the Church out of the world before the "Great Tribulation". Let me quote you from an e-mail I received from a Protestant who wants to join our church:

I am sincere in my search for Christianity, as it has always been. I would love to learn more about the Orthodox faith but I really don't know where to start. Any suggestions would be great! Here's a little background about me that might help explain how I came to believe Orthodoxy to be the true Church. I have been studying the Bible for 6 years now, first within the Pentecostal tradition and more recently in the Anglican tradition. I was "hood winked" by the Left behind (fiction based end times) and fell in with strict Protestants, disregarding Holy tradition of the Church. With serious study I feel the Bible can only be understood from an Orthodox perceptive.

Listening to new teachings can be the down fall of many in the time of Antichrist. For the deceiver will preach the Bible in order to deceive people, and put the poison of his teachings in a Bible covered pill. Hearing gossip is another offense. Maybe you say I do not take part in gossip but even hearing gossip is a sin. The desire to know the affairs of others is equated by St. James with murder and stealing, "But let none of you suffer as a murderer, a thief, an evildoer, or as a busybody in other people's matters." (1 Pet 4:15)

Listening to gossip leads us eventually to judging other people, forming wrong impressions about them and ultimately to spreading rumours about them. Listening to other people telling me what a certain person is saying behind my back is a very serious problem, especially with our young people. Someone comes to you and says this person is saying bad things about you behind your back, and you no more want to talk to this person. What you don't realize is that the person who is reporting to you is himself or herself talking about someone else behind their back! The solution for this? Tell the person who is reporting to you, "come and tell me this in front of that person." Remember that a person is innocent until proven otherwise.

Listening to vain and empty talk is another sin! Remember what the Lord said, "But I say to you that for every idle word men may speak, they will give account of it in the day of judgment." (Matt 12:36) Remember the story of the monk that was sitting chatting with the other monks, then, going to his cell, another monk saw him circling his cell several times. So, he asked him what he is doing. He answered, "I am getting rid of all the worldly talk we were talking about, because I don't want to bring it in with me into my cell!"

Finally, one very difficult offense to get rid of is listening to flattery! We all like it when people say good things about us but we forget what the Lord told us, "Woe to you when all men speak well of you!" (Luk 6:26) Flattery will be one of the most potent weapons that Antichrist will use to deceive people. The book of Daniel tells us that. In Daniel 11:21 we are told, "he shall come in peaceably, and obtain the kingdom by flatteries." Also in Daniel 11:32, "Those who do wickedly against the covenant he shall corrupt with flattery." And again in Daniel 11:33-34, "And they that understand among the people shall instruct many: yet they shall fall. Now when they shall fall, they shall be helped with a little help: but many shall cleave to them with flatteries."

Proper Use of the Ears:

Again here we should wean our ears from the bad things they have become accustomed to. Exercise yourself. Lent is a good time to teach your ears to fast from bad music, from gossip and all other unnecessary things like spending long time on the phone in idle talk.

Another thing we can do is to train our ears to perceive God in everything we hear. As an example, if you hear a beautiful tune, think of how much beautiful will be the music we will hear in heaven. Repeat in your mind the words of the beautiful hymn, "There David stands with harp in hand As master of the choir. Ten thousand times that man were blest That might this music hear. Our Lady sings Magnificat With tune harmonious and sweet And all the virgins sing their part Sitting about her feet."

Another exercise is meditating on the Passion of our Lord when we hear things. For example, if you hear the clock going ding dong, meditate on the sound of the nails being hammered into the hands of our Saviour.

Discipline of the Tongue:

The sense of taste has to be trained so that it does not dictate what one eats at all times. To have a liking for gourmet food all the time, and conversely, to have a disliking for humble foods is not the way of spiritual perfection. Remember our Mother Eve. One bite into the forbidden food had such a disastrous outcome. Amos 6:4 tells us, "Woe to you who lie on beds of ivory, stretch out on your couches, eat lambs from the flock and calves from the midst of the stall." Here it is not the food that is to blame but the life style.

Remember also the rich man, who "fared sumptuously

every day." Luke 16:19 emphasizes the word "everyday", for it is not a sin to eat delicious food once in a while, for example on feasts and when we have guests. For even the Father of the Prodigal sun ordered them to "bring the fatted calf here and kill it, and let us eat and be merry." (Luk 15:23) Even the Fathers of the desert broke their austere diet of dry bread, salt and water whenever they had a guest. They really splurged then; the master would tell his disciple, boil us a few lentils for the sake of the guest! St. Paul tells us, "everywhere and in all things I have learned both to be full and to be hungry, both to abound and to suffer need." (Phil 4:12) That means that I can enjoy a good meal but I can also endure hunger. I eat delicious food sometimes but I also eat humble food when I have to, for example during fasting. Train your taste buds to be content with whatever food there is.

Other Sins of the Tongue:

The tongue is not only the organ of taste, it is also the organ of speech. We are all familiar with the sins of speech, like swearing, lying, gossiping and taking the name of the Lord in vain. And I am sure that we all confess about these sins and get the proper advise from our Father in confession concerning them. What I would like to talk to you about are sins we do not confess about because most of us do not know that they are sins.

Talkativeness:

That talkativeness is a sin is obvious from what the Bible tells us. Here are some verses from the Old Testament about talkativeness: "In the multitude of words sin is not lacking, but he who restrains his lips is wise" (Prov 10:19) "He who has knowledge spares his words." (Prov 17:27) "A fool's voice is known by his many words." (Eccl 5:3) But the most stern warning about talkativeness comes from the Lord of Glory Himself, in Matthew 12:36-37, "But I say to you that for every idle word men may speak, they will give account of it in the day of judgment. For by your words you will be justified, and by your words you will be condemned." That means that every word said unnecessarily, we will have to account for on the day of judgment. That is scary!

The Fathers tell us that talkativeness is a sign of pride. A talkative person feels that he has lots of wisdom that he feels obliged to share with the world!

Talkativeness is the mother of gossip and backbiting and ruining of people's reputation. It is the root of arguments and boasting. A talkative person usually embellishes his stories with exaggerations and half truths to attract the admiration of the hearers. Young people spend hours talking on the phone, without feeling that they are doing anything wrong. But this is exactly what is meant by "idle words" of which we have to give an account.

A new twist to the long phone conversations is the infamous MSN conversations. Chatting on the internet is now the "in thing." You don't even need a computer anymore thanks to text messaging which is available on your cellular phone. The amazing thing is that some young people spend hours on MSN then pick up the phone to talk to the person with whom they were chatting.

The Fathers took this sin seriously, they cultivated the virtue of silence by various ways. Saint Arsenius once said, "Many times have I spoken and regretted it, but silence I never regretted."

The first step in combatting this sin is to realize that it is a sin. To ground in your mind the verse from Matthew 12 about "idle words." Next, you have to exercise yourself in silence. One of the Fathers used to put a pebble under his tongue to remind him to keep silent when he is attacked by the urge to talk.

Giving Advice:

Is giving advice a sin? Yes, in certain circumstances. First, if the advice is given without being asked for advice. And second, when you are not qualified to give advice. The problem is that when we are asked for advice, we instantly become experts on the subject even if we didn't know anything about it! Few are those who have the wisdom and the courage to say "I don't know."

It is unfortunate that many young people ask each other advice about important things like spiritual matters and "relationships." Instead of asking someone with knowledge, they seek advice from someone who does not have enough experience to be of any benefit to them. The Bible has something to say about this, "Can the blind lead the blind? Will they not both fall into the ditch?" (Luk 6:39)

Offering advice about serious matters is a grave sin, because you become responsible for the behaviour of the person to whom you are giving the advice. Of course if someone is asking you about homework or something like that, you have to give advice. But if your best friend tells you, about a person who is interested in him/her and what to do about it, don't start coaching your friend in something serious like this, because if this leads to sin, you will be held responsible.

Again if someone tells you he/she is using drugs, or smoking or masturbating, urge him/her to seek advice of his/her priest, rather than trying to help him/her, since you, yourself are in need for someone to help you with your own problems. You can encourage that person, by saying, "You know, I had a similar problem, and I went to Abouna, and he guided me out of this problem."

One thing you can do to help your friend, is to pray for him/her a lot. Write his/her name on a piece of paper and give it to Abouna to put it on the altar and ask him to pray for this person.

Sometimes the problem is so serious that I feel Abouna should know about it. But, what about the solemn promise I gave to my friend to keep the secret? One thing you can do is to tell Abouna that this is a confession you are making to him. This way he cannot mention that information to anyone, including the person who asked you. Abouna will pray for this person and ask God to guide him in how to approach this problem without divulging the information you gave him.

The Sense of Smell:

The sense of smell can provoke lustful thoughts and feelings. Strong smelling perfumes can produce lustful movements in the flesh. Ladies should not use very strong smelling perfumes so that they do not offend others. The Bible has something to say against wearing expensive and exotic perfumes. Amos 6:6 warns us by saying, "woe to you ... who anoint yourselves with the best ointments." and in Isaiah 3:24 we are told, "And so it shall be, instead of a sweet smell there will be a stench."

If I encounter a situation when a strong odour brings in thoughts of fornication remember Isaiah's saying that the flesh that you are lusting after will rot and stink.

The smell of food can also offend especially if you are fasting. If you pass by a hamburger or Pizza place, the smell can be very disturbing. Well, to quote ex-president Clinton, "Don't inhale!" Anba Abraam the bishop of Fayum, once had a compelling desire to eat stuffed pigeon (a delicacy in Egypt), so he told his servant to prepare it. When it was cooked, he told the servant to leave it. Whenever the servant asked him if he wanted it, he told him, "Leave it" After a few days it became rotten (there were no fridges in those days) then he told the servant to bring it to him. It smelled awful. The saint then told himself, "This is what your heart desires Abraam, go ahead and eat it!"

The Proper Use of the Sense of Smell:

If you smell a nice smell, always bring your thought to Mary who anointed the Lord with the sweet smelling ointment and how the "house was filled with the fragrance of the oil." (John 12:3)

The Sense of Touch:

The sense of touch played an important role in the original sin. When Satan disguised as a serpent came to Eve to tempt her, he asked her about God's commandment regarding the tree of the knowledge of good and evil. She answered the serpent, God told us, "You shall not eat it, nor shall you touch it, lest you die." (Gen 3:3) Eve must have touched the forbidden fruit out of curiosity and it must have felt so good and irresistible, so she plucked it.

We are all painfully aware that the sense of touch can lead to pleasant but unholy motions in both body and mind. For example, If, while sitting in a bus, my body comes close to the body of someone from the other sex, even though the bodies are separated by layers of clothing, yet, somehow, unholy feelings start disturbing my body and my mind. Sometimes we fight, but other times we surrender and even seek such situations.

Someone with trained senses would avoid such situations at all costs.

I remember a story in the Paradise of the Fathers about a young monk who was visited by his mother. He wanted to take her back to the edge of the village, and while going there, he had to cross a shallow river, and, out of courtesy, he carried his mother across. But, before doing so, he wrapped her in a blanket he was carrying. His mother was surprised and told him, "I'm you mother!" and the monk replied, "I am not afraid to touch your flesh mother, but touching you will bring to my memory other flesh that I touched in my foolish days."

St. Jude exhorts us to hate even the garment that has been defiled by the flesh. (Jud 1:23) We are all aware that the site of some garments on display windows or even catalogues can stir up unclean sensations in our bodies. Touching such garments can also stir up the same unholy sensations.

Touching certain parts of our bodies can produce intense sensual stimulation that is unchaste and unholy, and I know that a lot of young people from both sexes struggle very hard with these sensations.

In our social interactions we should be very careful with the use of the sense of touch, never using it indiscriminately especially with members of the other sex. Young people often hug and put their arms around people from the other sex in the name of friendship. Some may say, "I don't mean anything wrong." Others may say "I don't feel anything improper." But, what about the other person? If I stir in him or her improper senses, then I will have to answer for these. I can carry these exercises a step further by avoiding pampering my sense of touch with expensive clothes, using expensive lotions and cremes that make the skin softer. Moderation is the word.

The sense of touch is the vehicle through which we feel

unpleasant sensations or pain. A person with a well trained sense of touch will learn how to accept pain, even benefit from pain by remembering that the Lord endured pain for my sake. Theophan the Recluse gives some exercises in this regard. If I feel pain in my hand, I should think of the nails that went into the Lord's hands. If my back hurts, I should meditate on the 39 lashes the Lord endured on my behalf. If the pain is in my side, I should remember the spear, and if my head hurts, the crown of thorns should come to my mind.

CHAPTER FOUR

DISCIPLINE OF THE MEMORY
AND IMAGINATION

God endowed us with the ability to store information in our memory and to retrieve this information as will. God gave us memory in order to remember His commandments to us, "Remember all the commandments of the LORD, and do them." (Num 15:39-40) Through memory, the disciples remembered the words of the Lord Jesus when he was with them and later wrote them in the Gospels and the Epistles. The Gospels were recorded in the memory of the believers as an oral tradition long before they were written.

Another reason we were given memory is to remember all the good things that the Lord has done to us, "And Moses said to the people: "Remember this day in which you went out of Egypt, out of the house of bondage; for by strength of hand the LORD brought you out of this place." (Exod 13:3)

Satan can use both imagination and memory to tempt us to sin. Any object we perceive by our senses, leaves an impression in our memory that can be recalled, for good or for bad.

Sins of memory and imagination are even more dangerous than sins of the senses for these following reasons.

Sins of the senses are brought out by encountering an object that stimulates the senses, the sight of someone or something, a sound or a smell, etc.. That means that sins of the senses are brought about by external objects. On the other hand, through memory, one can instantly recall the same sensations he/she encountered through the senses, and dwell on them even in their absence.

Imagination can even add "special effects" to sensory objects stored in the memory making them more appealing and more exciting than they originally were.

Finally, senses go to sleep, but sins of memory and imagination can attack us even while we sleep, through dreams.

Sins of Memory

The remembrance of old evils. In the Liturgy, we pray that God may cleanse us form "the remembrance of evil that entails death." Remembrance of evil here means remembering either an evil that I did in the past or some evil done by another person against me.

Sexual Immorality:

The memory of sins committed in the past can come back to haunt us even after we stopped doing them. Some of the great saints of the desert suffered for many years of this. Saint Moses the Black was tormented by thoughts about his past evils for a long time. Amma Sarah, who was a nun contemporary with St. Macarius the Great, fought against these thoughts for 14 years, before the Lord granted her freedom from these assaults.

Sexually immoral pictures or movies that we see on TV or the Net are firmly imprinted in the memory and they usually come to offend us violently.

Anger:

I may have had an argument or a fight with someone, and even if we were reconciled, remembering what happened in the past can excite in us thoughts of anger and revenge that can be distressing. The devil can make things look and sound much worse than they really were. Many married couples live in misery because of this. A little argument in the morning before going to work is usually used by the devil very effectively. While at work, the devil causes the incident to be recalled in both their minds. Passionate feelings of anger and indignation are thus implanted in both their minds, so that when they come home, the little argument of the morning becomes a big fight that may rob both of them of their inner peace for weeks. How do you think divorces start? Some people even remember things deep in the past and recall them every time an argument happens. For example, a couple may be married for 10 years or more, and every time they have an argument, the wife reminds the husband of something he did (or didn't do) while they were on their honeymoon! The husband may also do the same and remind her of something her mother said while they were engaged!

Judging:

You may have witnessed or heard something done by another person and you immediately judge that person. You may have even repented and confessed about judging that person, but the matter is not closed. Every time you meet that person you remember what he or she did and you start judging that person once again in your mind. It is quite possible that this person too might have repented and confessed about whatever he/she did, he/she may have even forgotten it (as we should when we repent and confess) and yet you keep falling into the sin of judging him or her by the remembrance of evil.

Vainglory:

Sometimes we do something that seems good to us. For example, I may have helped reconcile two people, but later on I keep recalling all the "wise words" that I said to them, and revel and bask in the glory, telling myself, "Aren't I great?!" A Sunday School teacher may have been given grace in giving a lesson to his/her class. This grace is usually given for the sake of the children and not because of the excellence of the teacher, but he or she starts to recall every word that was said and the heart is filled with self gratification as if the words are coming from self and not from God.

Let me give you an exercise to fight this temptation. As soon as these memories start rising up in your mind, remember that the Lord used an ass (donkey) to rebuke the prophet Balaam. (Num 22:21-43, 2 Pe 2:14-15) Tell yourself, I have no more right to glory in my words than the donkey of Balaam!

SINS OF IMAGINATION

Sexual Immorality:

Suppose I work with a colleague from the other sex. The person is decent and he or she never flirts with me. Nevertheless, in my imagination I can commit the whole spectrum of sexually immoral sins with that innocent person. The person may be modest in his or her dress, but in my imagination, I parade that person in whatever flimsy ware that I fancy, or even undress him or her in my imagination, and commit fornication with that person repeated times. Now the reverse thing happens, whenever I see this person I start remembering the imaginary evils I commit with him or her. How do you think sexual harassment starts?

Another evil we commit by imagination is when we dwell on the sexual life of another person. Let me give you an example. You are sitting in a restaurant or a bus and you notice an elderly man and a young woman   sitting together chatting in a friendly manner. Immediately, in your imagination, you create an evil scenario, imagining the man to be her boss at work, and that she is his mistress ... The truth of the matter is that this is a girl sitting with her father, and you are falling not only into the sin of sexual phantasy but also into judging them.

Anger:

You have a mean boss at work who always puts you down, or a bully at school who always bothers you. You can't do anything about it in reality, so instead, you take revenge against that person in your imagination. You imagine yourself verbally abusing this person or even beating him into pulp. You may also parade in your mind various accidents that befall him/her like being killed in a car accident or falling from a tall building ... and all the time evil feelings of delight are filling your heart. What you don't realize is that you are committing murder in your imagination.

Judging:

If we disapprove of what someone else is doing, whether rightly or wrongly, we sometimes imagine ourselves giving a sermon to this person! Here we are delivering a passionate sermon, complete with verses from the Bible, rebuking that person for his/her evils and reminding him/her of God's judgement against those who do such evil things, and vehemently calling upon him or her to repent! What I don't realize is that I am committing the grave sin of judging others, and that God's judgement against me for doing that, will far exceed any judgement God may have on that person I am giving a sermon to in my imagination.

These thoughts can be so presumptuous that sometimes I indulge in giving a sermon to my Sunday School teacher, or my parents or even my Father in confession!

Vainglory:

The devil sometimes excites in my imagination visions about my "righteousness." I can indulge in imagining myself as a famous priest saving millions of souls by my "words of wisdom" and my "righteous life." Or imagine myself as a monk or a nun, exceeding all my peers in my ascetism ... When I was around 12 years of age, I often had fantasies about being a martyr! I reveled in my imaginary steadfastness in face of all the diabolic tortures that were inflicted upon my "holy" self!

Daydreaming:

No one can be free from daydreams. But to indulge in excessive daydreaming is a sin that one has to confess about. Daydreams are useless, they waste valuable time that can be spent in study or prayer or reading the Bible. Many students sit to study, go through the motion of opening the book, sharpening the pencil, but get immediately drown in their bitter-sweet fantasies.

One very real danger of these daydreams is that they often start as innocent fantasies, but they almost always end up as sexual fantasies. Girls often fantasise about their wedding! They imagine the wedding dress, the maids of honour, the gorgeous church in which the wedding is done, the sumptuous reception that follows... But, sooner or later this seemingly innocent fantasising will lead to fantasising about the... wedding night.

Love of the World:

Love of the world is enmity with God. (Jas 4:4) St. James tells us in the same verse that whoever loves the world is an enemy of God. In spite of this, we often indulge in this sin by imagining ourselves living in great palaces, wearing the latest trendy clothes, driving one of those dream cars. Cars are big on the minds of our pre-teen children. They talk about them, they paste their icons on the walls of their bedrooms and dream about them.

I was driving a group of our own youngsters from Toronto after an activity day they had there, and all they cared to talk about during the return trip was cars!

This temptation was one of the three temptations that the devil tried with our Lord, when he took Christ on a high mountain and showed him in an instance all the kingdoms of the world and their glory, and told him, "All these things I will give You if You will fall down and worship me." (Matt 4:9) Of course Jesus rebuked him, but how many times the devil tries the same trick on us by showing us all the worldly things he can give us if only we fall down and worship him. Every time we indulge in these fantasies, we are actually consenting to him!

Fantasising About Food:

This is especially dangerous when we fast! It is two weeks before the end of Lent and you fantasize about the sumptuous dinner you will have after the midnight mass. You can almost feel the food in your mouth and the smell in your nostrils. It is so real that your mouth starts to water! Even when you are not fasting, you suddenly start imagining yourself with a juicy mouth-watering hamburger or a fabulous ice cream, or whatever makes your mouth water. What you don't know is that you are committing gluttony in your imagination!

In the Old Testament, this sin assaulted the Israelites after they left Egypt. They told Moses, "We remember the fish which we ate freely in Egypt, the cucumbers, the melons, the leeks, the onions, and the garlic; but now our whole being is dried up; there is nothing at all except this manna before our eyes!"

(Num 11:5-6) God sent the people quails but punished them severely for their gluttony. "But while the meat was still between their teeth, before it was chewed, the wrath of the LORD was aroused against the people, and the LORD struck the people with a very great plague." (Num 11:33)

The Treatment

The first step is to recognize these sins as they are, and not think that they are harmless thoughts or fantasies. As such, you ought to mention them in your confession. As with any other sin you are fighting against, you need to pray and ask for God's grace to help you overcome them.

CHAPTER FIVE

PRESUMPTUOUS SINS

In Psalm 19:13, David prays saying, "Keep back your servant also from presumptuous sins; let them not have dominion over me. Then I shall be blameless, and I shall be innocent of great transgression."

What are these presumptuous sins? They are hidden sins. They are sins that are veiled with outward righteousness, so that they are not perceived as sins. They can also be actual virtues practised in a way not pleasing to God or not according to God's will. Sometimes these sins are called "Right hand sins" because they are sins that masquerade as virtues.

Examples of Presumptuous Sins

Self-reliance:

You hear a sermon and you feel your heart being pricked and a desire burns inside you to follow after righteousness. You start with great zeal, you fast, you pray a lot and you read the Bible. You feel an extra-ordinary energy moving you, that you mistakenly think is the grace of God, but alas, in a few days you fall flat on your back and you become worse than before. The problem is self-reliance. The solution is to go to your Father in confession and let him guide you. He will probably give you a modest program for readings, prayers and fasting.

Over-righteousness:

Even if you do it the right way and go to your Father in confession, the devil starts convincing you to do more than what your Father in confession told you to do. The devil starts telling you, "Abouna probably doesn't know your spiritual stature!" or "Abouna is delaying your spiritual growth." So, you start hiding your ascetic efforts from your Father in confession and only confess to him. Once you do this, the devil will actually help you in your ascetic endeavour, make you fast for longer hours, read the Bible excessively, pray more and more.

Why would the devil do that? In order to make your ascetic endeavour a goal in itself rather than a means towards perfection. You start to feel happy with how many hours you can keep fasting and how many metanoias you make. The Bible has a lot to tell us about this.

"Do not be overly righteous, nor be overly wise: why should you destroy yourself?" (Eccl 7:16)

"For I say, through the grace given to me, to everyone who is among you, not to think of himself more highly than he ought to think, but to think soberly, as God has dealt to each one a measure of faith." (Rom 12:3)

The devil used to come to Saint Antony, after he finishes his prayers and starts to give himself some rest and say to him, "Antony, wake up and pray!" But the wise Saint Antony used to reply, "I pray when I want to, but I will never listen to you." One has to be moderate in everything. This moderation is called by the Fathers The Royal Way, not swerving to the right (over- righteousness) or to the left (sinfulness)

It is for this reason that monks had a rule for prayer and fasting and readings assigned to them by their spiritual guide. You should always consult your Father in confession about your spiritual endeavours and ask him to assign you a rule for everything.

Punishing Yourself:

Sometimes in our do-it-yourself spirituality, we punish ourselves for the sins we commit. So, if you fall into a certain sin you increase your fasts, metanoias, or prayers and you think that you have dealt with the problem. Soon enough this will lead to:

Absolving Yourself:

For example, you are on a trip and the food served on the plane is non-fasting, so you allow yourself to indulge and justify it to yourself by the fact that you fast a lot and it is your right to have a break. What you don't realize is that the devil has made you take to yourself the power of binding and loosing which belongs to the priest. In reality, it is the devil that is binding and loosing you. He made you lose your spiritual director and he became your spiritual adviser! Again the Bible tells us something about this, "No one, when he has lit a lamp, puts it in a secret place or under a basket, but on a lampstand, that those who come in may see the light." (Luk 11:33) The Fathers of the desert tell us that what this means is, hide not your ascetic deeds from your spiritual adviser, do not practice ascetism secretly from your Father in confession.

The Delusions of Righteousness:

If you continue in this way, the devil will convince you that you are doing the right thing, that you are on the way that leads into life eternal, while in practice you are on the way to perdition, to losing your salvation. Again the Bible warns us against this, "Therefore take heed that the light which is in you is not darkness." (Luk 11:35) In Revelation 3:17, the Lord rebukes one of the bishops of the seven churches by saying unto him, "Because you say, I am rich, have become wealthy, and have need of nothing; and do not know that you are wretched, miserable, poor, blind, and naked." People who reach this stage are almost lost. Theophan the Recluse tells us that these people discover their state only after they die. It is of these people that the Lord says, "Many will say to me in that day, Lord, Lord, have we not prophesied in your name, cast out demons in your name, and done many wonders in your name? And then I will declare to them, I never knew you; depart from me, you who practice lawlessness." (Matt 7:22-23)

False Revelation, Visions, Dreams:

In order to confirm you in your delusion, the devil can sometimes make you "know things" before they happen! , or know the thoughts of people!

How can the devil do this? Very easy! He knows that your grandmother in Egypt is dying, so he puts the thought in your mind. You call Egypt and they tell you indeed that she is very ill. If you believe this, he will keep on telling you things in order to convince you that God is favouring you by these revelations, and fill you with the deadly sins of pride and self righteousness.

John Climacus tells us that the devil can implant a thought in someone's mind and reveal it to another to give him the illusion that he can read people's minds! Where do you think all those "Psychics" get their knowledge? From the devil. Actually most "Psychics" are really people possessed by demons.

Three monks were having "revelations" and they were arguing among themselves whether these revelations are from God or from the devil. They decided to go to Saint Antony the Great to ask him about these. While on the way to Saint Antony, the donkey they had with them died. They resumed their journey and when they reached Saint Antony, he told them, "Too bad that your donkey died!" They asked him, "How did you know about the donkey?" He told them, "The devil told me!" They told him, "You answered our question before we asked you."

Some people have visions of saints or angels. One has to be very careful before accepting these, because the devil can imitate these in order to ruin your spiritual life. The history of the desert Fathers is filled with horror stories about people who accepted these visions without discerning whether they are from God or from the devil.

One of these stories is the story of Heron, a monk that spent 50 years in asceticism and was brought to ruin by a false angel that appeared to him for a long time. He stopped going to church, and refused the advice of the other monks, who advised him to tell the Abbot about this. In the end the "angel" convinced him that he was going to be taken alive to heaven like Elijah. The poor man went to say goodbye to his fellow monks, who tried in vain to convince him that this is the devil, but he would not listen. The "angel" took him to a mountain and convinced him to jump, and of course he fell to his death. The Abbot would not allow the psalms to be chanted for him. He considered him as one who committed suicide.

Another "angel" appeared to another monk for three years. The cell in which he lived was shining with the light of the "angel", so that he did not need to light any candles! After three years, the "angel" gave him a vision of "Paradise" showing him the Jews sitting in the bosom of Abraham, while the Christians were being tortured in Hades, He left Christianity and became a Jew.

There were wiser monks though. To one "Gabriel" appeared with a message from God! He told him, "You must have come to the wrong cell, for I am a sinner unworthy of revelations, but the monk next door is a saintly man." "Gabriel" disappeared in smoke! To another monk "The Lord" appeared and told him to worship him, but he said, "I don't want to see the Lord on earth, I want to see him in heaven." Again, the false "Lord" disappeared in smoke.

Now these are things that happened to monks centuries ago, but the devil is still using the same techniques even today, with great success. Many years ago, I noticed that one of the servants has stopped coming to church and having communion for a long time and I decided to visit him and ask him about the reason for this. He simply told me,

"Pope Kyrillos appears to me every Sunday and gives me communion!" Another servant from out of town, told me that something was bothering his conscience. Since I was not his Father in confession, I advised him to confess to his own Father in confession. The next morning he called to tell me that "Pope Kyrillos" came to him in a dream, asked him to confess, then gave him the absolution. He asked me if this is good enough, but I told him, I still suggest very strongly, that you go and confess to your Father in confession, and tell him about this dream.

There are true apparitions, but there are also false apparitions, in the same way that there is real money and there is counterfeit money. And the proper way to handle revelations, apparitions and dreams, is to consult with your Father in confession.

A spiritual person will always deem him/herself unworthy of these revelations. Dreams are totally under the control of the devil. God spoke to certain people through dreams, but these can be counted on the fingers and they were saints and prophets, not sinners like us. We should not give much weight to dreams. Saint Antony once said, "He who believes in dreams is the toy of the demons."

False Gifts:

In a later stage, the devil may actually give you "spiritual gifts" like healing gifts, or people ask you to pray for them and in a short while, their problems are solved. The devil can give someone a headache, and cause it to go away when you pray for him! Or cause a problem for someone, and later solves this problem when you pray for that person. An example of this kind of trickery is given to us in the life of Saint Pachom. There was another monk training with him under Abba Palaemon, who used to taunt St. Pachom that he is not striving enough. As a proof of this, that monk used to walk on burning coals without being hurt! St. Pachom felt very discouraged because he could not do the same. One day, the monk came to him and told him, Today, I am going to jump into a furnace and will not be burned! He jumped into the furnace and was consumed by the fire.

Saint Pachom was very shaken by this and he went into the desert and started to pray, telling God, "This is too difficult for me!" But God sent an angel to comfort St. Pachom and tell him, "Because of your humility, God will grant you discernment, so that the devil cannot trick you this way, and you will be able to help others who will become your disciples."

Where do you think all those TV "Healers" get their gifts from? It's from the devil. The Bible tells us that the devil can cause illnesses. Possessed persons healed by the Lord often had blindness, deafness, epilepsy or other ailments caused by the demons. In the Book of Job, we are told that Satan "struck Job with painful boils from the sole of his foot to the crown of his head." Satan can cause someone to be temporarily blind, and then allow the "healer" to "heal" him! Why? Because both the healer, the healed and the spectators are deceived by these false "miracles."

False Consolation, False Tears:

Sometimes the devil, in order to confirm you in your

delusion will give you a false warmth in your heart, even false tears that start coming down when you pray. This is very easy. He just tells his demons not to disturb you or tempt you in order that you may be deceived and think that you are doing the right things.

Here is a true example of how he does that. Long time ago, I met two young people who were living together in sin. They used to tell me, "Abouna, we pray the Agpeya together, and we read the Bible together, so how can this be wrong?" There was an old song that had this lyric, "It can't be wrong, when it feels so right!" Every time I hear this song I think to myself, "The devil himself must have written this song!"

The Peace Before the Storm:

This is another trick that the devil uses in order to ambush young people into sin. It goes like this. A boy meets a girl and they start meeting behind their parent's back. They are afraid to tell their Father in confession, so they ignore this part in their confessions. "It's only friendship" whispers the devil in their ears. They spend hours together without having any unseemly desire towards each other. They don't kiss or touch (because the devil told his demons not to attack them.) They fall into the trap of false security. They can meet in a room by themselves, even sit on a couch without doing anything unholy (again because this is the script written by the devil.) One day, they are sitting on the same couch like they used to do for so many months, and suddenly, the demons attack from every direction. Feelings of lust suddenly swamp them. Totally unprepared, they fall into sin.

The War of the Opposites:

This is another trick of the devil by which he tries to spiritually exhaust us, and make us easy prey. He plants two opposed thoughts in our mind. They are both good thoughts, but they alternate without ceasing in our mind. Each one has its own arguments, supported by the appropriate verses from the Bible. You go on and on trying to find out which one is from God and which one is not. The truth is that they are both from the devil. This he does to drain you and engage your mind in fruitless pursuits in order to weaken you and make you easy to attack. The easiest solution to this dilemma is to talk to your Father in confession.

The Spiritual Progress War:

The devil may make you over-anxious about your spiritual progress. "You are not making any progress, change your Father in confession," he whispers in your mind. What we don't know is that God hides from us the fruits of our strife, even unto the last day of our life. He does this out of love for us , for if we see results, we will immediately attribute the results to our own piety and not to Grace, and thus lose all what we gained from our strife to pride and self-righteousness.

When the Lord brought Israel into the promised land, He told them "The LORD your God will drive out those nations before you little by little; you will be unable to destroy them at once, lest the beasts of the field become too numerous for you." (Deut 7:22) The Fathers explain this to us by saying that these "nations" symbolize our sins. The Lord does not want to destroy our sins quickly, lest the beasts of the field, pride and self- righteousness, increase in us and devour us.

The Lord also gave us a parable that we should not expect to see results for our strife, "And He said, The kingdom of God is as if a man should scatter seed on the ground, and should sleep by night and rise by day, and the seed should sprout and grow, he himself does not know how." (Mark 4:26-27) If you have a house plant it will grow every day, but if you try watching it to see if it grows, can you see it? So it is with your spiritual life, do not expect to see results because God hides the results from us for our own good.

Secondary Sins:

The Fathers tell us that every demon going out to fight against the faithful has two "assistant demons," one on his right hand and one on his left hand. The one on his right hand is called the demon of pride, and the one on his left is called the demon of despair.

If the principal demon succeeds in tempting you to sin, the demon of despair takes over. He starts rebuking you harshly in order to make you despair from your salvation. You may think that this is your conscience, or God rebuking you because of your repeated failure, but you are mistaken. The Fathers tells us that when God rebukes, He rebukes gently and lovingly, never harshly.

If you resist the temptation, the demon of pride starts to put thoughts of self-righteousness in your mind, by telling you, "You really became experienced in fighting this sin,!" in order to make you lose the victory you just scored by the grace of God. The demon of despair sometimes implants thoughts of blasphemy in our minds, or thoughts of fornication, while we are standing in line to take communion. He then rebukes us very harshly trying to make us despair from salvation.

A monk went to his Abba, very distressed because of thoughts of blasphemy that were attacking him constantly. His Abba told him, ignore those thoughts and say, "These are your thoughts not mine, may your blasphemy be upon your head."

The treatment of these tricks is to be aware of them, expose them and fight them. Go to your Father in confession and reveal the thoughts to him. The Fathers tell us that as soon as you reveal the thoughts to your Abba, they will disappear.

CHAPTER SIX

THE PURSUIT OF VIRTUES

Virtues are the fruits that everyone is required to bring forth in his/her spiritual journey towards Christian perfection. "Every tree which does not bear good fruit is cut down and thrown into the fire." (Matt 3:10) That is what the Lord tells us about the importance of these fruits. However, before we proceed any further, let us listen to what the Lord further tells us, "Abide in me, and I in you. As the branch cannot bear fruit of itself, unless it abides in the vine, neither can you, unless you abide in Me. I am the vine, you are the branches. He who abides in me, and I in him, bears much fruit; for without me you can do nothing." (Joh 15:4-5)

So, the first rule of bringing fruit is this, "without me you can do nothing" No one can produce fruit by his/her effort only. It is God Who makes us fruitful. God is like a farmer who owns a land and Who hires a servant to look after the land. The land and the seeds are owned by God, even the fertilizer is owned by God. God sends the rain and the sunshine required for the cultivation. But the hired servant has to till the land, put the seeds, pull out the weeds and put the fertilizer, then harvest the fruits of his labour. But, in spite of his work, the hired servant has no merit in what he does and so are we as the Lord tells us, "So likewise you, when you have done all those things which you are commanded, say, We are unprofitable servants. We have done what was our duty to do." (Luk 17:10)

Virtues do not just happen. One has to train for them in the appropriate way. Virtues are often likened to a ladder with many steps that leads from earth to heaven. Some of the virtues are at the bottom of the ladder; others are at the top. The Fathers tell us that we cannot "skip" but rather should ascend the ladder of virtues in an orderly fashion.

At the bottom of the ladder are the two basic virtues of obedience and patience. At the top of the ladder are the higher virtues of humility and love. Love is considered the highest of all virtues. It is often called, "the all-encompassing virtue". One that has love will have all the other virtue also. In the training for virtues, we are advised to take them one at a time. Once we have finished our training in one we should start on the next step up the ladder.

Virtues are cumulative. Training in one virtue make it easier to acquire the next one. For example, if you train yourself in obedience and patience, meekness will be at your grasp. And once you have mastered meekness, you are at the doorsteps of humility, and so on. Training needs a trainer or a coach. No one can make it in athletics without a coach, neither can one be a successful "athlete for Christ" without a coach.
Your coach is your Father in confession. He should be in charge of your training program. If you have read and understood the last chapter, then you will surely have discovered the perils of trying to do it on your own.

Obedience and patience are considered pre-requisites for all the other virtues. You cannot have fruit in any other virtue if you have not mastered these basic virtues. The reasons given for this is that if you have no obedience, you will not follow the instructions given by the trainer! And, obviously, there will be no progress. Likewise, without patience you will not be able to persevere in your training until you bring forth fruit.

In the parable of the sower, our Lord tells us, "But the ones... on the good ground are those who, having heard the word with a noble and good heart, keep it and bear fruit with patience." (Luk 8:15) In the remainder of this chapter we will be considering some practical "techniques" in the training for obedience and patience.

Obedience:

Obedience is subjecting your will to the will of another. The

Fathers took great pains in training their novice disciples in this very important basic virtue. We are all familiar with Saint John Colobos (the short), who was told by his trainer to take a stick, put it in the ground and water it every day! Another Abbot told a novice to stand at the door of the monastery and bow himself down to everyone entering through the door, begging him, "Please pray for me for I am a leper!" This may seem ludicrous to you and me, but that shows you how seriously those Fathers of the desert took training for virtues. And before passing judgment on their "techniques", please look at the results or the fruits. After years of toiling to water the stick, the stick budded and brought fruit, and the "master" took the fruits to the other monks telling them, "Come eat of the fruit of obedience."

To be truly obedient, you do not have to agree with the request. And the more objectionable the request, the more reward you will get for your obedience. When God asked Abraham to offer his only son Isaac as a sacrifice, Abraham never stopped for a moment to inquire if this request was "reasonable". He just did it. Of course God never intended to have Abraham slay his son. God gave Abraham this seemingly "unreasonable" request to test his obedience, and he was generously rewarded for this obedience.

In the same manner, you do not score points for being obedient in things that you like or agree with. You score points when you practice obedience in things that you disagree with or don't like to do. For example, if your dad tells you, "Get dressed because we are going out to have dinner in your favourite restaurant" and you say "Yes sir!" I do not think that you will be rewarded by God for this kind of obedience! But if dad asks you to help him in shovelling the snow or mowing the grass, or mom asks you to help with the dishes and you say "Yes sir" or "Yes Mam" that is when you get rewarded.

One important aspect of obedience is that it should be

"In the Lord" "Children, obey your parents in the Lord, for this is right." (Eph 6:1) The request has to be according to the teachings of the Bible, because, "We ought to obey God rather than men." (Act 5:29)

The Training for Obedience:

Having consulted with your Father in confession, and sincerely prayed to God to initiate you, and sustain you in this endeavour, you can now start the work of training. Start early in the morning, by reviewing all the chances that God gives you to practice this wonderful virtue. Start by making a resolve to be obedient throughout the day to your parents, your teacher, or your husband or wife. Say to yourself. "I am not doing this for them but for God's sake" Once you have made this resolution, do it without hesitation. It may be hard in the beginning, especially if your dad or mom ask you to help in some errand during your favourite soap opera! Force yourself to do it for the sake of succeeding in your effort to implant this wonderful virtue in your soul.

If the errand is boring you to death, just try to entertain yourself by saying to yourself, "Hey, my parents think that I am being obedient to them. They don't know that I am doing this for my own good!" And if the errand is very objectionable, console yourself by saying to yourself,

"I am doing this to get a reward from God not from my parents (or my husband or wife)."

Do not ask yourself if the request is reasonable or not, just do it for the sake of acquiring the virtue of obedience. As a matter of fact, the more unreasonable the request, the more quickly you will acquire the virtue. A classical example given in the wonderful little book "The Way of the Ascetics" is this: Your wife tells you, "Take the umbrella for it is going to rain today". You look outside and it is sunshine, not a single cloud in the sky, and you tell yourself, "There is no way it is going to rain today!" Well, maybe you are right, but this is a wonderful chance to practice obedience for obedience's sake. And if people give you strange looks for carrying an umbrella on a day like this, smile and say to yourself, "They have no idea what I am doing this for!"

To be obedient is to be prompt in doing what you are asked to do. The two classical answers that young people give when asked to do something are these, "Do I have to?" and "In a minute!" Of course that minute takes forever. If you are serious about your training in the virtue of obedience, you have to force yourself to be prompt.

A story that illustrates this is the story of a monk called "Mark the Calligrapher" who lived in a monastery with other monks. The monks made a complaint to the Bishop that the Abbot of the monastery loves Mark more than the others! The Bishop came to investigate, and asked the Abbot about this, and he said, come and I will show you. The Abbot went knocking on the doors of the cells of the monks and each one of them said, "I am coming," only to open the door minutes later. When he knocked on the door of Mark, the door was opened instantly. The Abbot took the Bishop inside to where Mark was sitting to work. There was a manuscript that Mark was inscribing, and in it was an unfinished vowel. Mark heard the knock on the door and did not wait to finish the vowel he was inscribing before opening the door. When the Bishop saw that he said, "Not only do I understand why you love him but now I love him too!"

How long should I do this? If you are sincere in doing these exercises in the way described, it will probably take you no more than two weeks to ingrain this wonderful virtue in your soul. It will be difficult in the beginning, but later on, it will be effortless. Obedience will become a second nature to you!

Patience:

The importance of patience is given to us by the Lord Himself. Speaking of the Great Tribulation that will come before His second coming, the Lord tells us, "And you will be hated by all for my name's sake. But he who endures to the end will be saved." (Matt 10:22) And again, "By your patience possess your souls." (Luk 21:19) In speaking of these last days that precede His second coming, the Lord tells us, "when the Son of Man comes, will he really find faith on the earth?" (Luk 18:8) and again, "because lawlessness will abound, the love of many will grow cold." (Matt 24:12) This means that faith and love will be weakened in those perilous days, but "he who endures (is patient) will be saved." And by patience one can possess (or preserve) his soul. Patience may be the virtue that saves one in those last days. The book of Revelation, which speaks to us about the last days, again stresses the importance of patience in overcoming the difficulties of those last days. "Here is the patience of the saints; here are those who keep the commandments of God and the faith of Jesus." (Rev 14:12) But patience is not only important for survival in the last days, it is important for our spiritual survival today. "For you have need of endurance, so that after you have done the will of God, you may receive the promise." (Heb 10:36) Even after doing the will of God we still need patience in order to receive the promises of God. "Therefore be patient, brethren, until the coming of the Lord. See how the farmer waits for the precious fruit of the earth, waiting patiently for it until it receives the early and latter rain." (Jas 5:7) Patience is what keeps us going, and struggling towards perfection, in the hope for the "precious fruit." Again, "Let us run with endurance the race that is set before us," so tells us Saint Paul (Heb 12:1).

The Training for Patience:

Like with any other virtue, ask the guidance of your Father in confession. Then pray to God asking Him to guide you in using the many occasions that he grants you every day in order to practice patience. Do not, however, imitate the person who prayed to God saying, "God please give me patience, and I want it right now!"

God, in His love towards us, gives us plenty of chances to practice and acquire this important virtue of patience. Unfortunately, because we are not "tuned" towards God properly, we fail to realize these opportunities and most of the time we miss taking advantage of them. For example, you are out of a job and it has been two months now. You have sent hundreds of resumes to various places; you have been praying fervently, but, alas, not a single response. You start blaming God and asking, "Why is God doing this to me?" The answer is this, God is giving you a golden opportunity to practice patience. It is the easiest thing for God to give you a job right away. But an instant job will not lead you into the Kingdom of Heaven, patience will. So, God gives you a chance to practice and acquire patience, and the sooner you do it, the sooner he will give you that job!

More often than not, we are absorbed in the problem, trying to find out why is God doing this, or trying to solve it on our own without ever realizing why God in His mercy is sending us this problem. Saint Paul tells us in Romans 8:28, "we know that all things work together for good to those who love God." That means everything that happens to us is for our own good, if we love God. A wise person then, as soon as something happens that he does not understand, should ask himself, what message is God sending me? What virtue does God want me to practice now?

Saint Paul again tells us in Hebrews 12:11, "Now no

chastening seems to be joyful for the present, but painful; nevertheless, afterward it yields the peaceable fruit of righteousness to those who have been trained by it." What this means is this, even though initially, the problem may not be something that brings joy to us, yet if we use it as an exercise in patience, the fruits will give us peace and joy. "My kids are driving me crazy!" said a mother to me, and I told her, "You are lucky! Your kids are the school of virtue which will lead you to eternal life, you should thank God for them!"

The Bible tells us again and again that "problems" are good for us because they teach us patience. "Knowing that the testing of your faith produces patience. But let patience have its perfect work, that you may be perfect and complete, lacking nothing." (Jas 1:3-4) That means, trials and tribulations create patience in us, but we are warned that this "work of patience" has to be perfected (through practice) before we ourselves reach our goal of Christian perfection.

Saint Paul tells us the same thing in Romans 5:3-4, "tribulation produces perseverance (patience); and perseverance, character" Once we get it into our heads that all difficulties that are sent our way are meant for our own good, that we may through them exercise ourselves and be experienced in patience, we will have no problem acquiring this saving virtue. Having recognized the "problem" as an opportunity to practice patience, I have to prepare my mind for using this opportunity to its fullest potential, or "let patience have its perfect work" as Saint James tells us. If it has been two months without an interview, I should resolve within my mind, "Even if it takes two years without a job, in order to acquire perfect patience, I will endure it." Comfort yourself by saying, "God loves me, and that is why he wants to give me the incorruptible instead of the corruptible, the heavenly instead of the earthly and the eternal instead of the temporal."

Strengthen yourself by saying, "The sooner I resolve within myself to 'endure to the end' the sooner will God solve the problem for me." One of the saints once said, "You cannot describe to someone the taste of honey, he has to taste it himself." What this means is, you have to try this yourself. You have to exercise yourself in this virtue faithfully before you feel the sweet results of your exercise. And the results are worth it, for they will endure with you. Once you have completed this exercise successfully, the experience will remain with you till the end of your life. You will always go back to the same resolve that you initially showed and remember the sweet fruits of that resolve; how God after giving you the grace of patience throughout your tribulation, has lifted your tribulation and has given you more than you ever hoped or asked for. You are now well grounded in patience and ready to move on to the next step on the ladder that leads to Christian perfection.

CHAPTER SEVEN

MEEKNESS

Meekness is a "fruit of the Spirit" (Gal 5:23) The Lord Himself exhorts us to meekness by saying, "Take my yoke upon you and learn from me, for I am gentle (meek) and lowly in heart, and you will find rest for your souls. For my yoke is easy and my burden is light." (Matt 11:29-30)

How can we imitate the meekness of the Lord? Let us see what the Bible tells us about His conduct, "He will not cry out, nor raise his voice, nor cause his voice to be heard in the street. A bruised reed he will not break, and smoking flax he will not quench." (Isa 42:2-3) This is how Isaiah the great prophet describes the Lord prophetically. The picture we have here is of someone who is quiet, speaks in a low voice and is peaceful in dealing with others. In other words, someone who has subdued anger.

Saint Paul exhorts us in Romans 12:18, "If it is possible, as much as depends on you, live peaceably with all men." Today, anger is a very serious problem, in people of all ages. We have road rage, flight rage and rage without any cause. Movies and TV, computer games and even cartoons condition anger in people who watch them. No wonder that "Anger Management" courses have become a big business.

Degrees of Meekness:

The Desert Fathers give us degrees of meekness. They correspond to the degrees of fruitfulness that the Lord spoke about in the parable of the sower, "But others fell on good ground and yielded a crop: some a hundredfold, some sixty, some thirty." (Matt 13:8)

The first degree is not to repay evil with evil. Saint Paul exhorts us in Romans 12:17, "Repay no one evil for evil." Saint Peter tells us the same thing, "Not returning evil for evil or reviling for reviling, but on the contrary blessing, knowing that you were called to this." (1 Pet 3:9) Our Lord was a perfect example of this, "Who, when he was reviled (insulted), did not revile in return; when he suffered, he did not threaten, but committed himself to him who judges righteously." (1 Pet 2:23)

The second degree is to accept the insult without losing your internal peace. Some people refrain from repaying evil for evil but inside thy are boiling with anger. They are filled with thoughts of anger and the desire for revenge. These people have stopped short of the second degree of meekness. We have examples among the Fathers of the desert to illustrate that this second degree of meekness is possible.

Saint John Colobos was very famous, so that many people came to him to hear him. Another monk was envious of his fame, so he told him in front of those who gathered around him, "John, you are like a whore, exhibiting her body in front of her lovers." John answered him, "Brother, you see my outside and say this about me, what would you say if you saw my inside?" The people around him asked him, where you agitated internally by the insult? He answered them, "What John feels on the outside is what he feels on the inside."

Some monks from Syria, hearing about the fame of Egyptian monks came to an Egyptian monastery to see how the monks conducted themselves. It was the custom of the Egyptian monks to eat early if they had guests, in order not to force their own asceticism on others. So, when the table was set for the guests from Syria, they thought within themselves, "Those Egyptian monks are lax, we persevere without food till the end of the day, and here they are eating at the ninth hour!" The Abbot, perceiving within himself their thoughts decided to teach them a lesson. There was an old monk going around the table distributing bread to the brethren, so, when he came to the Abbot to offer him bread, the Abbot suddenly smacked him on the face so forcefully. The old monk continued to offer the bread with the same expression he had on his face before being smacked. The Syrian monks then prostrated themselves before the Abbot saying, "Forgive us Abba, for we can persevere without food longer but we cannot control our passions the way you do." The third degree is the person who is insulted and feels grieved that he caused a brother (or sister) to sin.

The Training for Meekness:

Once again, having taken permission of your Father in confession, turn to prayer. Ask the Lord to teach you how to be meek like Him. Tell Him, "Lord, you have said, learn from me for I am meek, teach me this meekness, so that I can find rest unto my soul."

The next step is to reason with yourself in this way. Peace is a gift from the Lord to me, for it was He Who told us, "Peace I leave with you, my peace I give to you." (Joh 14:27) Every time you give in to anger, you are losing your peace, the precious gift that Christ gave to you personally. It is like taking this gift of Christ and throwing it away. Imagine if some bishop gave you a gift, would you throw it into the street? If the answer is no, how much more the gift of Christ, that you actually throw away each time you give in to anger.

Once you have put this disposition firmly in your mind, do the following exercise suggested by Theophan the Recluse: In the morning, after you have said your prayers, review in your mind all the situations that may arise and that may lead you to lose your peace. Imagine the worst case scenarios in your mind and then ask yourself, even if this happens, is it worth throwing away the precious gift of Christ? If you have done the previous step properly, your answer will be an emphatic NO! Resolve then within yourself that you will not let any of the things that you reviewed in your mind, should they happen, to disturb your peace.

My friend, let me tell you, it works! Years ago I read this exercise in a book called "Unseen Warfare" and decided to try it. The results exceeded my expectations. I give this exercise to many people. Those who take it seriously are amazed by the results.

A mother of four, who took the exercise seriously and followed it religiously, later told me, that her kids ask her, "Mom, are you sick or something?" She is not sick, she is just enjoying the gift of peace that Christ gives to each one of us, and which unfortunately we throw away ever so easily.

But the ultimate weapon to be confirmed in this state of internal peace can only be reached if you take the next step: "Pray for those who spitefully use you and persecute you." (Matt 5:44) Nothing confirms the peace of Christ in your heart like praying for people who hate you and hurt you. Again, take my word for it, it works. And if you do this with zeal, you will be able to reach the state of "loving your enemies," which is commanded by the Lord in the same passage of Matthew 5:44.

People who have taken this admonition seriously, have been rewarded by a lasting peace that no one can take from them. Many years ago I knew a young man in Egypt, who had a very high position in a large organization. He was a Copt. Being a Christian in Egypt can sometimes be hazardous for your health, especially if you hold a coveted position!

This young man who worked in a remote area of Egypt, had a boss (vice president of the company) who was very fanatic. He made it his goal in life to kick out this Christian guy in order to bring someone of a different religion in his place. For years, he conspired to frame him in one crime or another. Many a time would the police come to investigate him for an anonymous complaint. One time the police chief (who was not Christian) told him, "someone around here wants to really harm you."

When the attempts to put this young man in jail failed, his boss conspired to kill him! The young Copt learned that from the sympathetic police chief who told him in confidence, that someone had been paid money to kill him and that he should be careful not to go out after dark.

Throughout this ordeal, the young man prayed and read the Bible. Every time he opened the Bible, there was Matthew 5:44 before him. He kept asking the Lord, Lord, do you really expect me to pray for this man who made my life miserable and now wants to kill me? Time and time again the answer in his heart was an emphatic yes.

After struggling with the idea, he decided to blindly follow what the Bible said. So, he started to pray for his boss. In the beginning he prayed only with his lips, not his heart. But, as he persevered in this exercise, something wonderful started to happen. He found himself truly praying for this person with his whole heart.

Feelings of animosity towards that person were soon replaced with feelings of pity! He started to think in himself, if I had not been born as a Christian, I would probably have done what this person is doing. A new meaning for the Lord's saying, "yes, the time is coming that whoever kills you will think that he offers God service." (Joh 16:2) He started to feel sorry for the man. "This poor man thinks that he is doing the will of God by persecuting me, just like Paul of Tarsus, who thought that he was doing God a favour by destroying the church." The young man said to himself, "It could have been me doing this, if it weren't for the mercy of the Lord who chose me to be one of His own." He started thanking the Lord for allowing him to be the persecuted rather than the persecutor. He started doing good deeds to his persecutor, and earnestly asking God to forgive him.

One day, the president of the organization called the young man in his office and told him, "I found out what is happening to you and what .... (the vice president) has been doing to hurt you and I know the reason why he was doing these things to you. And I wanted you to be the first to know that I have fired him!" There was no joy in the heart of the young man. He felt sorry for the children that will wake up to find their father unemployed. You too my friend can have unshakeable peace in your heart, if you take your Bible seriously, and follow these exercises diligently.

CHAPTER EIGHT

CHASTITY

Why did God create sexuality in man? Is it for procreation only? Bishop Moses, in an old article of Al-Keraza, wrote the following. God created sexuality for the sole purpose of preservation of the race in animals. That is why animals are only sexually active for a few days or a few weeks every year. This period of sexual activity is called "the period of heat". During this period, the female produces a certain scent that arouses the male. Animals mate during this period, and after that they are not sexually aroused. It is not so in humans, for they are the only members of the animal kingdom that are always in heat! So why is this? Bishop Moses gives us the answer, it is because God wanted humans to share and enjoy a holy kind of love that is likened to the love of Christ and His Church. Saint Paul says, "This is a great mystery, but I speak concerning Christ and the church." (Eph 5:32) This is how St. Paul speaks about the mystery or Sacrament of marriage. It is a great Sacrament, but only because it mirrors the relationship between Christ and the Church. But as holy and as great is the use of sexuality within holy matrimony, its use outside marriage is so abhorable. Saint Paul adds, "Marriage is honorable among all, and the bed undefiled; but fornicators and adulterers God will judge." (Heb 13:4). And again,

"Flee sexual immorality. Every sin that a man does is outside the body, but he who commits sexual immorality sins against his own body." (1 Cor 6:18) Sexuality within marriage is uniquely blessed as a sacrament that emulates the love between Christ and His bride, the Church, while sexuality outside marriage is distinct from any other sin, because it defiles the image of love between Christ and the Church. "Do you not know that your bodies are members of Christ? Shall I then take the members of Christ and make them members of a harlot? Certainly not!" (1 Cor 6:15)

Saint Athanasius the great has a wonderful analogy to contrast sexuality within and outside marriage. He tells us, If a soldier goes out to war and kills twenty of the enemy's soldiers, he is decorated. But, if in the time of peace he goes out in the street and kills one man, he is condemned. It is the same action, done in different circumstances with completely opposite outcomes.

There is no more evidence that human marital love is blessed than the fact that when God wanted to give us a description of the love between Christ and the Church (or the human soul, the unit of the Church) He gave us this in one book of the Bible called the Song of Songs. It is a book that is often misunderstood and often attacked even as pornographic. But, there is nothing sinful or pornographic about the marital relationship, because it simulates the love between Christ and the Church. "Husbands, love your wives, just as Christ also loved the church and gave himself for her." (Eph 5:25) This is where marital sexuality differs from sinful sexuality. Sinful sexuality is concerned with taking, grabbing, exploiting, self gratification, while marital sexuality is about giving. Marital sexual love should be modeled on the love of Christ to the Church, Who "gave himself for it". Marital sexual love is about self-giving not grabbing or taking, and that is what makes it holy, because it is Christ-like.

"Flee sexual immorality" says St. Paul, but someone may say, "Easier said than done!" And I agree, for chastity is the most elusive virtue. You think that you have reached it only to be overthrown once again in its pit.

The Bible tells us about the perils of fornication, "Do not be deceived. Neither fornicators, nor idolaters, nor adulterers, nor homosexuals, nor sodomites, nor thieves, nor covetous, nor drunkards, nor revilers, nor extortioners will inherit the kingdom of God." (1 Cor 6:9-10)

In this sweeping sentence, the Bible condemns all sorts of sexual immoral acts. Fornication means pre-marital sex, while adultery means extra-marital sex. They are two degrees of one sin, except that the punishment is different! A fornicator commits sin against his/her own body and also against his or her partner, while an adulterer commits sin against his/her own body, the partner and the spouse. Note that homosexual acts are also condemned. "Effeminate" and "abusers of themselves with mankind" refer to both participants in a male homosexual act.

Lesbianism is also condemned in the Bible, "For this reason God gave them up to vile passions. For even their women exchanged the natural use for what is against nature." (Rom 1:26)

The Lord adds to this list of sexually immoral acts, all sorts of lustful passions, "Whoever looks at a woman to lust for her has already committed adultery with her in his heart." (Matt 5:28) It goes without saying that a woman looking with lust upon a man, or a person looking with lust upon someone from the same sex will be as guilty. Today, the list has gotten bigger, for pornography became such a major problem with even little children. Pornography leads to sexual phantasies and masturbation.

While condemning these immoral acts, the Bible does not explain to us how we can fight against them. For this we have to draw on the experience of the Desert Fathers. They are the experts on the subject.

Covering the basics

According to the Desert Fathers, there are some preliminary steps that one has to take before his quest for chastity. Here is what they say:

Control Your Stomach:

It is very unlikely for someone who is overcome by gluttony to be able to achieve chastity. That is the consensus of opinion of the Fathers. A full stomach, ignites the passions of the flesh. It makes sense that if one is not able to control his passion for food, he will not be able to control the more difficult sexual passion.

Control Your Sleep:

Oversleeping, say the Fathers, also contributes to increase in the sexual drive. One has to fight against oversleeping in order to avoid falling into sexual sins. The Bible actually advises us against oversleeping. Proverbs 6:9 exhorts us, "How long will you slumber, O sluggard? When will you rise from your sleep?" And again Proverbs 20:13 advises us, "Do not love sleep, lest you come to poverty."

Control Your Temper:

The Fathers insist that if we cannot control anger, we will not be able to control our carnal desires. The Fathers classify sins and they tell us that anger and fornication belong to the same category of "excitable sins". One of the Fathers even tells us that the demon of anger and the demon of fornication are one and the same. One who is easily excitable to anger will be easily excitable to the dictates of the flesh.

Here is what the Fathers tell us about this:

As a person progresses in mildness and patience of heart, so also does he in the purity of body. And the further he has driven away the passion of anger, the more tightly will he hold on to chastity.

There are two more factors that I would like to add from my experience with young people, and these are:

Drinking:

Alcohol is a very potent stimulus of the passions of the flesh. Resistance to sexual sins dissipates when one allows himself to drink even moderately. The great Shakespear realized this and wrote in one of his plays describing the effect of wine on sexual behaviour, "It creates the desire but takes away the performance!" Through the many years I have served as a priest, I have heard many horror stories about drinking and fornication, but this one stands in my mind. It concerns a 16 years old girl of German descent, who was very religious. She used to come and baby sit my children when they were little. We were very pleased with her, since she read the Bible to our children, a rare find even in the seventies. One day her mother told her, "You don't have a life! Why don't you attend the neighbourhood New Year's party?" She agreed. Someone gave her this funny tasting orange juice and she drank it. Not only did she lose her virginity on New Year's Eve, but she realized later that she became pregnant. The perpetrator was a married man with kids. The mother refused to allow her an abortion. She was a retired nurse, she went back to work to allow her daughter to keep the baby. Six month later, she died of a heart attack.

Dancing:

Dances are the most common way for "relationships" to start. Again, it suffices here to tell one of the many horror stories that sticks up in my memory. It was the eighties, and I had to go to the U.S.A. to serve instead of another priest on vacation.

After communion, I was approached by a 13 years old girl who wanted to confess. I took her to the office of the priest I was covering for, and she went on crying and sobbing. I tried to calm her down, asking about the reason for her tears. Finally she started talking, "I had sexual intercourse". It turned out she went to a dance (her parents were "enlightened"), danced with a 15- year old boy, and before the night was over she had lost her virginity.

"Did he rape you?" I asked, "No Abouna, I wanted it as much as he did. With the music and the lights and our bodies close to each other, I had no desire to resist." That was her answer.

Let us return now to the Fathers. They tell us that even if we control overeating, oversleeping and anger, we still need another virtue before we can attain to chastity. They tell us, "You covet chastity, then covet humility, because without humility you cannot obtain chastity." The most common problem in the fight against desires of the flesh is self-reliance. "I am going to do this and this, and I will have victory!" Let me give you a dictum about spiritual strife, anything that starts with "I" is doomed to fail! Unless we abandon relying on ourselves, we will fail and fail and fail. No one was ever able to control carnal desires by self-control! Here is what one of the Fathers tells us in this regard:

We are unable to acquire chastity through our efforts, unless, while exerting ourselves constantly, we are taught in the school of experience that it is granted to us by the bounty of divine grace. For this reason, one should persevere tirelessly in his efforts, so that he will deserve to be freed from the assaults of the flesh, thanks to the divine gift. He must not believe that he will attain by himself the bodily chastity that he seeks.

In trying to explain this concept to young people, I use this analogy: Imagine a little child trying to reach a toy placed on a table. The table is too high for him to reach, so he tries to stand on his tiptoes but it doesn't work. He starts jumping up and down but he cannot reach. He even tries to climb on some object or another, only to fall and hurt himself. Totally frustrated, he starts to cry. His father, who has been watching him, then reaches for the toy and gives it to him. The little child did not get the toy by his own efforts, but the efforts inclined the heart of his father to help him.

The problem is that we do the same, we try and try and fail and then in our frustration we cry, and God will give us a respite from the fight. But sooner or later, the devil will suggest to us that we did that by our own effort. Once you admit this thought, you lose everything and you are back to square one. The most amazing thing is that this keeps repeating itself, and we keep on repeating the same mistake without ever learning why we keep falling back. Abbot Chaermon has this to say about this state of affairs:

For each one of us who contends against the spirit of fornication, it is a notable victory not to expect relief through our own efforts. That is not easy even for the experienced. For when purity smiles on them ever so slightly, they immediately flatter themselves in the depths of their conscience by a pride that subtly slips in. They think that they achieved this by their own diligent zeal. Thus, it is necessary for them to be deprived of heavenly protection and to be oppressed by these passions which the divine power had extinguished, until they realize by experience that they are unable to attain the good of purity by their own strength and toil.

Again and again the mercy of God will give us a glimpse of purity, and again and again we will fall into the trap, stealing the work of the grace of God and ascribing it to our own effort. This goes on and on until we finally realize that only God's grace can give us purity.

What can I do when I fall into this trap? First of all you

have to realize that God allows these falls for your own good. Second, acknowledge that your pride is the reason for your fall and ask God to give you back His grace. Here is what Abbot Chaermon says:

When someone has begun to rejoice over an extended period of purity believing that he can no longer fall away from his virtue, he will start boasting within himself. But, when having been abandoned by the Lord for his own good, he realizes that the state of purity in which he placed his confidence is abandoning him, let him return at once to the Author of his integrity. One has to be trained by God through these oscillations until he is confirmed by the grace of God in the purity he is seeking.

These "oscillations" may take years and years before reaching true chastity. But these oscillations are useful because they give us experience not only in fighting against fornication but also against pride and self-righteousness.

Do not be dismayed if you have been falling again and again in this trap, for it is difficult even for the experienced as Abbot Chaermon tells us. Amma Sarah, one of the great women ascetics of the desert, fought against fornication for fourteen years until God granted her freedom from this passion, and so did Saint Moses the Black.

Finally, when we are humbled by the many times we thought that we have prevailed only to discover that we did not, we fall into the state of the "littleness of heart" and we admit defeat and our total inability to win this war. It is then that God intervenes and grants us a reprieve out of pity. Now that we have been exceedingly humbled by our dismal performance, grace surprises us, the war ceases and the temptations do not bother us anymore. Then we feel a wonderful warmth in our heart, because now we know with great certainty that this "sudden death" of the sinful movements of the flesh is a gift of grace totally unrelated to our efforts.

The Struggle for Chastity:

Like any other virtue, prayer should be the first mainstay of the struggle to attain chastity. Show God that you really desire chastity and that you are not paying Him lip service. You should develop hatred for impurity, because you cannot fool God by asking Him to give you purity while deep inside you enjoy sin.

But, what if you cannot reach this stage? Some young people come to me saying, I really want to repent, but I cannot bring myself to hating sin. Well, go to God honestly and tell Him about your predicament. Say with the Psalmist "Create in me a clean heart O God."

The Prayer of the Oblations, which is said in the Morning offering of Incense is a beautiful prayer asking God to reward those who have offered unto God. But it also asks God to reward "those who desire to offer but have none." Take your cue from this prayer, throw yourself at the feet of the Saviour and say to Him, "Lord, I am one of those who desire to offer but have none. I wish I could offer a true desire for purity but, I am unable to."

Saint Augustin was once in this stage, he used to pray saying, "God, I want to repent but not now for I have not had my fill of pleasures!" God caught up with Saint Augustin, and the man that lived in sin for 30 years, became a bishop! Beware of making vows of chastity to God, or promising Him anything! Because you will be promising something you have no control over in the first place.

Next to prayer, you have to put a sincere effort in the fight against impurity. It does not make any sense to pray to God to give you purity while you watch pornography, or give in to evil thoughts without attempting to arrest them.

Do not look for immediate results for your "efforts" for this is self- righteousness. Only God knows your progress.

Fight as much as it is in your power without worrying about the end result. God will mark you for effort and not for results. God knows that you are no match for the devil, and does not expect you to prevail over him. God just wants you to fight courageously even if you lose in the end.

Abbot Theophan the Recluse gives a nice analogy for this. He says,

"If a soldier is surrounded by his enemies and goes on fighting until he is seriously wounded in the battle, he is decorated as a hero. But if he sees the enemy around him and raises the white flag and surrenders, he is considered a traitor and is punished accordingly."

Actually, you may feel that you have lost, but God will count this as a victory. There is a nice story to illustrate this from the "Life of Antony" written by Saint Athanasius. Saint Antony was tempted by the devil in so many ways, he appeared to him in the shape of beasts to frighten him, in the shape of women or gold to tempt him, but St. Antony resisted. Finally, the devil appeared to him in his ugly shape and started beating him up until he lost consciousness. When his disciple found him in this state, he carried him and put him in the church of the nearest village. When Saint Antony regained consciousness, he looked up and saw the ceiling of the church open and the Lord Jesus appeared to him sitting on the throne of His glory. Saint Anthony felt sorry for himself and said to the Lord, "Where have you been Lord when the devil was beating me up?" The Lord answered him, "I was right beside you Antony, but you were doing so well that I decided not to intervene so that you don't lose your reward!"

You see, Saint Antony saw defeat in the beating that the devil gave him but the Lord saw in it a victory worthy of a reward. The moral of the story is this, just fight, don't worry about the results of the fight.

The Wiles of the Enemy:

The enemy tries to put as many obstacles in our way or trick us to quit the fight. Here are some of his famous tricks.

You resist for a long time then you are overcome, so he suggests to you that since all is lost, why not indulge some more and try later. Wrong! Since you fought with courage, all is not lost, you did not lose the war, you just got wounded in the battle. Do not give in and wallow in your impurity because that is treason! If you lost while fighting, you deserve a reward! To give in to his suggestion that "all is lost" and that "it doesn't matter anymore" is to help him rob you of your reward! So, stand up and resume fighting and do not give in to the thoughts of defeat, and the Lord, who endured the temptations of the devil, will pity you and help you.

The other trick is this. He suggests to you that since in the end you are going to lose, so why bother fighting? He tried this one on a monk and the monk told him, "One blow for you and one blow for me!" It is like a boxing match. You try to give your opponent as many blows as you can regardless of how many blows you receive. Only at the end of the match will you know the score!

Another famous trick is this. You fall into sin, you feel guilty and want to go back to God and ask for forgiveness. The devil rebukes you saying, "How dare you show your face or talk to God after what you have done!" And then he suggests to you, "Wait for a few hours or a few days until you are "clean" and then pray! Wrong! You come to God as you are. When the Prodigal Son decided to come back, he came immediately. He had the stench of the swine he had been living with all-over him. He did not wait to put clean clothes on him. It was the Father who took away his filthy clothes and gave him a clean robe. The Father did not disdain the stench of his son. He was overcome by His love for his son who was dead and is now alive.

He ran and embraced him even though he had the stench of sin all-over him.

Father Lev Gilet, an Orthodox monk noted for his spiritual writings, once wrote this, "You must be certain that in the same moment that you are committing sin, God loves you." The devil may suggest otherwise but he is a liar.

So, as soon as you fall, immediately go on your knees before your loving Father and tell Him, "Father, I have sinned against heaven, and before you, and am no more worthy to be called your son." Immediately you will feel the warm embrace of the Father and His loving kisses. Once more you are on your feet fighting again with courage. Needless to say that this initial act of repentance does not take the place of confessing to your Father in confession.

Another trick he will try is this one. He comes and says to you, "How many times you have done this? Do you think God will go on accepting you every time you come running back to Him?" The answer is yes! For when Peter asked the Lord how many times he should forgive his brother every day, the Lord answered him seven times seventy. Don't you think the Lord Who expects us to forgive each other seven times seventy every day will give us the same chance? As many times as you fall, come back to God. He will never turn His back on you.

A lay person went into a monastery and asked one of the monks, "what makes you different from us who live in the world?" and the monk answered, "We fall, then we rise up, then we fall, then we rise up then we fall then we rise up!" You see, we are all in the same boat!

Do not over-grieve if you repeatedly fall, for Theophan the Recluse tells us that this is a sign of pride. Consider this as a remedy sent to you by God to teach you humility. One of the Fathers of the desert said, "Defeat with humility is better than victory with pride." And Saint Isaac the Syrian tells us this, "Some please God by their virtues, others by their contrite and broken heart." So, even if you fall into sin and show a contrite and broken heart, this will please God too.

Some people get discouraged because they have been trying for a long time without success. Someone asked Abbot Chaermon, how long it takes a person to gain chastity? He answered,

Whoever has withdrawn himself from every useless conversation, has put to death all anger, concern and worldly care, does not over eat or over sleep, and yet does not believe that he will obtain it by these efforts, but rather by the mercy of the Lord, for such person it is not impossible to attain purity in six months.

How long do you think it will take someone who has not yet reached this level of spirituality to attain purity? Six years? Think of Amma Sarah, who fought for fourteen years before being granted victory. Sometimes we can trick the devil! Like the monk who used to get very hungry and is tempted to break his fast, who used to tell himself,

"Let us pray two more psalms, then we eat" and afterwards, he says, "Just two more psalms and surely this time we will eat!" and he goes on and on. Suddenly he is not hungry anymore, because the devil gave up on him! We can use the same technique in fighting the urge to sin, say to yourself, "Let us sleep tonight and see what happens tomorrow!" This way we can postpone falling until we are completely exhausted, and gradually our staying power will increase and the frequency of our falling will decrease.

Finally, what should we do when God grants us chastity? Let us listen to what Abbot Chaermon tells us in this regard:

One who has acquired chastity should rejoice at the purity that has been bestowed upon him and should understand that he has acquired it not by his own effort and vigilance but by the protection of the Lord. And he should understand that his body will persevere in this as long as the Lord mercifully permits it. … He should never trust in his own virtue, nor be weakened by a flattering sense of security knowing that he will be sullied (become dirty again) if the divine protection departs from him for a little while. Therefore, in all contrition and humility of heart, one must pray ceaselessly for perseverance in this purity.

CHAPTER NINE

DISCERNMENT

Discernment of the spirits is one of the gifts of the Spirit mentioned in 1 Corinthians 12:10. The Bible exhorts us to discern the spirits, "Beloved, do not believe every spirit, but test the spirits, whether they are of God." (1 Jn 4:1) It was the gift King Solomon asked God to give him, "Therefore give to your servant an understanding heart to judge your people, that I may discern between good and evil." (1 King 3:9)

Saint Antony ranked discernment as the virtue that should be coveted more than any other, because without discernment, the practice of other virtues may not be pleasing to God.

Discerning of Thoughts:

There are many thoughts that move within the human soul. These thoughts may have one of three origins:

1. From man himself, as we are told in Psalm 94:11: "The LORD knows the thoughts of man, that they are futile."

2. From God (the Holy Spirit abiding in us) as we are told in (Matthew 10:19-20) "But when they deliver you up, do not worry about how or what you should speak. For it will be given to you in that hour what you should speak; for it is not you who speak, but the Spirit of your Father who speaks in you."

3. From the devil as we are told in John 13:2: "And supper being ended, the devil having already put it into the heart of Judas Iscariot, Simon's son, to betray Him." and also in Acts 5:3: "But Peter said, Ananias, why has Satan filled your heart to lie to the Holy Spirit and keep back part of the price of the land for yourself?"

Discerning the origin of the thought can be very difficult since a thought can be coming from God, to be quickly followed by a thought coming from Satan. An example of this is shown to us in Matthew 16:

Simon Peter answered and said, You are the Christ, the Son of the living God. Jesus answered and said to him, Blessed are you, Simon Bar-Jonah, for flesh and blood has not revealed this to you, but my father who is in heaven. (Matt 16:16-17)

From that time Jesus began to show to his disciples that he must go to Jerusalem, and suffer many things from the elders and chief priests and scribes, and be killed, and be raised the third day. Then Peter took him aside and began to rebuke him, saying, Far be it from you, Lord; this shall not happen to you! But he turned and said to Peter, Get behind me, satan! You are an offense to me, for you are not mindful of the things of God, but the things of men. (Matt 16:21-23)

As you see, in St. Peter's mind, a thought from God was quickly followed by a thought from Satan. St. Peter could not discern the origin of the thoughts because he had not yet received the Holy Spirit.

Although the Bible exhorts us to "try the spirits whether they are of God," we are not given an exact method for discerning the thoughts. Again we have to go to the Desert Fathers seeking their experience in this matter. Here is a summary of what they say:

1. Examine the thought to see if it is filled with the fear of God.

2. Is it filled with goodness towards every one?

3. Does it agree with the witness and actions of the Lord and the Apostles?

4. Does the thought evoke peace and tranquillity? or is it surrounded by anger, bitterness and turmoil? The most pious thoughts should be suspected if they deprive us of our inner

peace.

Many a time we are lead to believe that we are being moved by the zeal of the Lord while we are actually succumbing to anger, condemnation and partiality. This happens to us time and again because we neglect this important step of examining the feelings surrounding the thought. An example of how God speaks to us is given to us in 1Kings 19, God wanted to talk to Elijah the prophet, and we are told,

A great and strong wind tore into the mountains and broke the rocks in pieces before the LORD, but the LORD was not in the wind; and after the wind an earthquake, but the LORD was not in the earthquake; and after the earthquake a fire, but the LORD was not in the fire; and after the fire a still small voice. (1Kg 19:11-12)

The voice of the Lord is a still small voice, not a great wind that breaks the mountain, or an earthquake nor a fire. A thought that is surrounded by feelings of pride, stubbornness, selfishness, confusion, anxiety, violence, envy and partiality, then it is certainly from God. Thoughts that are from God fill us with serenity, joy and humility.

5. Does the thought come with a sense of urgency about it? Do you feel compelled to do it right away? If so, then be very careful, for most probably it is from the Tempter. Stirrings of the Holy Spirit come to the soul gradually and gently and not impulsively.

Saint Macarius the Great once had a thought to go and visit the monks in the surrounding area. He kept the thought within him examining it for two years lest it be from the devil!

You may do all these steps and still the devil can fool you! The most important test of where the thought is coming from is to reveal your thoughts to your Father in confession. Never trust in your own judgment especially concerning important matters. I personally learned this the hard way! Here is how it happened.

Long time ago in the early years of my priesthood, we were starting a new project in the church that caused a lot of controversy and alienated several members of the congregation. Two weeks before the start of the project, I had this thought constantly in my mind that love and harmony are better than projects. I thought that God was telling me to stop the project and try to reconcile the people that were against it. I spoke to the members of the Board about what I decided to do, when one of them told me, "Abouna, you taught us always to reveal our thoughts to our Father in confession before deciding anything, have you consulted your Father in confession?" I really felt ashamed that I forgot this very important step. I called my Father in confession and revealed my thoughts to him and he told me, "This thought is from the devil!" He also told me that His Grace Bishop .... was going to be in town shortly, and that I should consult with him before making any decision. I went to meet His Grace and told him about my thoughts, and he told me, "It is from the devil" I felt really humbled. I asked him, how could your Grace and my Father in confession discern the thought and I couldn't? He smiled and said, "We just have more experience!"

The Bishop told me, "The devil wants to scuttle the project, so he stirs up controversy about it and then appealing to you in the name of love and harmony, he convinces you to stop it. But here is what you do, you go on with the project and in a short while the controversy will die when the people see the project come to completion." That incident taught me a great lesson about never trusting in my own judgment without consulting. I hope it will teach you the same.

Discerning the Will of God:

Sometimes one gets into a situation when he is unable to take a decision easily. For example, you get accepted into two universities, one in your home town and the other is out of town but is more famous. Or you have a job but you get an offer of another job in another city and you can't make up your mind. It is these situations when we sometimes ask, "What is the will of God for me?" Knowing the will of God can be very difficult, but not if we follow the methods of the fathers.

But, before we get into this, let us ask ourselves, why is it important for me to know the will of God?

Saint Paul tells us in Romans 12:2, that the will of God is good, and acceptable, and perfect. The will of God is perfect, it lacks nothing, it is good for me in satisfying my spiritual, physical, psychological and emotional needs. God knows the future and therefore he knows what will be good for me in the long term.

My own will, on the other hand, is anything but perfect. I probably look for benefit in the short term without considering the long term. And even if I wanted to consider the long term I may not be able to, since I cannot predict what will happen to me even next week.

It is for these reasons that a wise person should always seek the will of God in whatever he does. But, how can I know the will of God? Theophan the Recluse tells us that in order for God to reveal His good, acceptable and perfect will to me, I have to renounce my own will. That means, I have to prove to God that I am really seeking His will.

Sometimes we ask God to reveal His will to us but deep inside we have already made up our minds. Sometimes we seek the will of God, as long as it agrees with our own will. If we act in this way then God will not reveal His will to us.

Theophan the Recluse gives us this "parable." He says, if you have a glass full of vinegar, and you want to put honey in that glass, you must first throw away the vinegar, wash the glass, put it out in the sun for a few hours until the smell of the vinegar disappears, and then put the honey in it. The vinegar here is our own will which is selfish, short sighted, and unlike the will of God, is not perfect, good or acceptable. The honey is the will of God. And, unless we bury our own will, God will not reveal His will to us, because we will actually be mocking God by asking him to reveal to us His will while our own will is already made up.

How do I do this? There is an exercise for this called neutralization of my will. The theory is this. I always have a bias either for or against anything I am considering. For example, if I get an offer for a job that will give me more money, I may have a bias towards that job, which will make me blind to the bad aspects of this job. Or, I may face a situation in which I am asked to accept something that I don't like, and that makes me overlook the many good features of that thing. These likes and dislikes are usually based on a first impression, that I usually re-enforce by ignoring the other side of the coin, and the remedy is to do the opposite.

Let us take an example. I have been accepted in a good university in my home town, but I have an offer from another university that is far from home. The lure of "freedom" makes me ignore the many negative aspects of going to study far from home. If you really want to know what is the perfect, good and acceptable will of God in this matter, I should neutralize my bias, by intentionally identifying and even magnifying the negative aspects of that far away university.

For one, I will be far from my family and friends. I will feel lonely, with only strangers to talk to. There is no church near that university, but I will have to travel for hours to find a

Coptic church. I will lose my Father in confession, to whom I could always come for help, but who will be far away from me, and so on.

Of course these negative aspects are true but you were ignoring them because of "freedom" away from home and parental scrutiny. Any one who is serious can do this exercise in a few days. The result will be that you will find yourself neutral to the two proposals, each one has its good and bad aspects.

The same can be applied to the situation where you get an offer of a job that promises thousands of dollars more, but at the expense of taking your children away from their schools, their friends and their Sunday School, and moving away from your service in the Church and from your Father in confession.

The first step then is to neutralize the bias by seriously identifying the negative aspects and giving them as much weight as the positive ones. Then and only then, you can go to God to ask Him to reveal His good and perfect and acceptable will to you.

The next step is to go to your Father in confession and ask him to pray for you, so that God may reveal His will to you. This act of submitting yourself to your Father in confession is an act of humility, a very necessary pre-requisite for God revealing His will to you.

If you feel afraid that God will chose the one option that you do not favour, then you have not done your home work the right way, the bias is still there. And if you go to your Father in confession asking him to pray for you but, subconsciously, you wish that God will choose one option over the other, then you have not done your homework well. It may well be that God will actually choose the one option you favoured before you neutralized your will, as I will show you in the next example.

A young man that I knew in Egypt before coming to

Canada, wrote me a letter complaining that although his parents and his siblings are all in Canada (as immigrants), he has been consistently refused permission to immigrate by the Canadian embassy.

I wrote to him telling him, maybe it is not the will of God that you immigrate to Canada. I then explained to him how to seek to know the will of God and how to neutralize his own bias in this respect. He accepted my advise and started thinking about the benefits of not immigrating to Canada.

He told his wife, if we stay in Egypt, our house will be the place where my parents and siblings come when they want to visit Egypt. And, since we have good jobs here, we don't have to start from scratch if we go to Canada, writing exams only to be told that we do not have "Canadian experience." We could always visit Canada and enjoy being with our family, and thus have the best of both worlds. They both went re-enforcing this until they became convinced that staying in Egypt is not such a bad idea after all, especially if this is the will of God for them.

In his next letter he wrote me, "The same day we felt free from the bias and it didn't matter anymore for us whether we immigrate or stay in Egypt, was the day we received a telephone from the Canadian embassy telling us we were approved and have to do the medicals in order to receive our visas. The beauty about doing this exercise, is that every time you are faced with the same situation, you go back to the same routine. It will be very easy for you not to think too much about what you ought to do, but rather neutralize or "bury' your will so that the perfect, good and acceptable will of God may be revealed to you.

There are some words of caution that I would like to tell you. Do not try to cheat! Sometimes we seek the will of God but when God reveals His will to us, we don't like it. Some people would go to another priest hoping that changing the priest may change the will of God! The other problem is that we ignore the will of God completely and seek our own will, just praying to God to give us what we want. This can be disastrous especially in the matter of marriage.

The late Bishop Poemen of blessed memory once told me a story about a young man who always came to the Bishop because of marital problems with his wife. One day the Bishop in frustration asked him, "Have you prayed at all before marrying this girl?" and the man told him, "I prayed everyday for six months!" The Bishop asked him, "What did you say to God?" The man said, I said, "God please let me marry this girl!" Accepting the will of God as the best option for me, is a difficult concept for many young people. One young woman told me once, "I will accept the will of God in everything except for marriage!" And I asked her Why? She said, "Because I know that the will of God will be that I marry a deacon who teaches in Sunday School who will be boring to live with!" I told her, "Can't God choose for you a deacon who teaches in Sunday School who will be fun to live with?"

Another young man who attended a retreat where we spoke about "the will of God in my marriage," stood up objecting violently to what I was proposing. He told me, "When it comes to marriage, I want to be the master of my own destiny!" I told him in response, "If you ignore the will of God in the process of choosing your spouse, you will become the master of your own disaster!"

I like to give to our young people this parable; your life is like a boat where two people have to work, one has to row and the other has to hold the rudder (the device that directs the boat to turn right or left). A wise person would hand the rudder to the Lord and say, "Lord, hold the rudder and I will row!" Unfortunately, many times we insist on holding the rudder and we want God to row!

One benefit of accepting the will of God as your preferred

option is that, whatever life brings your way, you will have no fear, knowing that if God willed this for me, it is certainly good, perfect and acceptable, even if in the short term I don't like it.